Slow Cooker

Slow
Cooker

Over 70 of the
best recipes

Sara Lewis

hamlyn

A Pyramid Paperback

First published in Great Britain in
2006 by Hamlyn, a division of
Octopus Publishing Group Ltd
2–4 Heron Quays, London E14 4JP

ISBN-13: 978-0-600-61464-7
ISBN-10: 0-600-61464-6

A CIP catalogue record for this book is
available from the British Library

Printed and bound in China

10 9 8 7 6 5 4 3 2

Notes

Standard level spoon measures are used
in all recipes
1 tablespoon = one 15 ml spoon
1 teaspoon = one 5 ml spoon

Both metric and imperial measurements are
given for the recipes. Use one set of
measurements only, not a mixture of both.

Some manufacturers specify that their slow
cooker should be preheated before use. Refer
to the instructions for your specific slow cooker
and follow the settings and timings suggested,
if required.

Use free-range medium eggs unless
specified otherwise.

Use semi-skimmed milk unless
specified otherwise.

Pepper should be freshly ground unless
specified otherwise.

Fresh herbs should be used unless stated
otherwise. If unobtainable use dried herbs
as an alternative but add just a pinch.

A few recipes include nuts and nut derivatives.
Anyone with a known nut allergy must avoid
these. Children under the age of three years with
a family history of nut allergy, asthma, eczema or
any other type of allergy are also advised to avoid
eating dishes that contain nuts.

Contents

Introduction

Slow cooking is the new cooking revolution – an apparent backlash against years of tasteless microwave-blasted instant food. Slow cookers have been around since the 1970s, but, unlike the hostess trolley or teasmaid of the same era, are now making a serious comeback. If you don't already own one yourself, the chances are your mother had one. So retrieve it from the back of the cupboard and dust it down, or think about buying one. Offering a time-saving, economical, healthy and versatile way of cooking, the slow cooker is simply a must for modern living.

The benefits of slow cooking
- Enhances the natural flavours of food
- Saves time and money

Burgundy Beef Stew with Horseradish Dumplings – comfort food at its best.

- Allows food to cook unattended with no fear of burning or spoiling.
- Offers 'convenience food' with a difference – home-cooked food with none of the colourings, additives or preservatives of commercial convenience food.

Time-saving
The beauty of slow cooking is quite simply that an electric slow cooker cooks food slowly for up to 8–10 hours, so, once you have added the basics to the pot, you can leave the food to bubble completely unattended. It won't burn, boil dry or dry up, leaving you time to get on with your life. Just 15 minutes or so first thing in the morning putting on a hearty homemade soup, meaty casserole or vegetarian main meal will be time well spent. What could be better than to be welcomed home at the end of an exhausting day by the aroma of a supper ready to be dished up?

Economical
Slow cooking is economical and environmentally friendly. Why use a large conventional oven for one item when you can switch a slow cooker on? It uses much less fuel, costing only the price of an electric light to run. In addition, because foods are cooked so slowly, cheaper cuts of meat or inexpensive dried pulses can be cooked to perfection.

Healthy lifestyle
Slow cooking is healthier, too, being ideal for dried beans, lentils and split peas – just make

A slow cooker can double-up as a bain-marie (water bath), making it ideal for cooking crème brûlée and other custard dishes.

sure you soak all pulses first and boil all soaked beans for 10 minutes before adding them to the cooker pot. Pulses are not only a good source of fibre but also provide protein, which is essential for those following a vegetarian diet. Furthermore, because vegetables and fruit are cooked and served in their own juices, vital minerals and vitamins are not lost.

Versatile

A slow cooker is very versatile. Yes, they make great casseroles, but they can also be used to cook pot-roast joints and make soup, side dishes and desserts. Fill the slow cooker pot with warm water and it can be used as a steamer for cooking fish or steamed puddings, or as a bain-marie (water bath) for baking custard-style desserts. You can even use it for making cheese or chocolate fondues, chutneys and conserves, or mulled wine.

Keep the slow cooker on the work top at all times, and once you get into the routine of putting a meal on to cook before you go out, you will find it hard to imagine how you ever managed without one.

Who needs a slow cooker?

Families with young babies or children – it can be exhausting coping with a young family. You will invariably be woken at some dreadfully early hour, so why not put it to good use and get the supper on? Then, when you have completely run out of steam by early evening, supper is ready and waiting! Cooking in a slow cooker also leaves you free to enjoy your time with older children when they get back from school in the afternoon.

Students – a slow cooker is ideal for cooking budget-priced cuts of meat or vegetarian suppers, so you will be able to cook a healthy, nutritious supper for less than a trip to the nearest take-away outlet.

Working couples – it may seem a tall order to get the supper on before you go out to work, but once you have tried it, it can be more appealing than rushing around preparing a meal when you're tired in the evening.

Retired people – a slow cooker can be put on while you enjoy a day out on the golf course, shopping or just relaxing. While it is a good way to cook cheaper cuts, a slow cooker is also perfect for informal entertaining, too.

Choosing a slow cooker

With their new sleek designs, the modern range of slow cookers will not look out of place in even the trendiest of kitchens.

Slow cookers have lost their old-fashioned image and are now bang up to date with a range of different sizes and styles. Look for the trendy new chrome- and black-finished machines lined with a black ceramic pot, alongside the more traditional country-style cream, white or green machines. If you are choosing a slow cooker for the first time, go for a model with a removable pot as these are much easier to serve from and wash up.

All slow cookers work on a low wattage and all consume similar amounts of electricity. They are so well insulated that, even though they will be on for hours, your kitchen will not fill up with steam, they will not need topping up with water or require any attention.

What capacity?

Slow cookers are usually marked with their total capacity on the packaging. While this is important, the actual cooking, or working, capacity is more crucial.

- A standard slow cooker has a total capacity of 3.5 litres (6 pints) with a maximum working capacity of 2.5 litres (4 pints). This is ideal for a family of two adults and two children.
- A slightly larger, 5 litre (8¾ pint) slow cooker with a maximum working capacity of 4 litres (7 pints) will suit four adults.
- An extra large, 6.5 litre (11½ pint) slow cooker is ideal for a family of six as it has a maximum working capacity of 4.5 litres (8 pints).

A slow cooker must be used half-full for best results, so do bear this in mind. The extra large size is great value for money, but unless you have a big family, you may need to increase the recipe quantities that you would normally make. This could mean eating the same supper for two days or freezing the extra portions.

Timing controls

Different makes of slow cooker vary slightly with regard to the design and nature of their control panel. All have a 'High', 'Low' and 'Off' setting, while some may have 'Medium' or 'Warm' as well. All the recipes in this book have been tested on 'Low' or 'High' settings. If you wish to speed up or slow down the cooking time, use the timings (above right) as a guide, although they may need to be adjusted.

Variable timings have been provided for the majority of recipes, with many ready in 8–9 hours or 8–10 hours. This means that the food will be ready to eat by the first time given, but can be left cooking without spoiling for an extra hour, or even two hours, depending on the recipe.

Cook on 'Low'	Cook on 'Medium'	Cook on 'High'
6–8 hours	4–6 hours	3–4 hours
8–10 hours	6–8 hours	5–6 hours
10–12 hours	8–10 hours	7–8 hours

(timings taken from the Morphy Richards slow cooker instruction manual)

The 'Warm' setting is ideal if you are running late. The heat will be low enough to keep the food hot without it spoiling. Only use this setting for food already being cooked in the slow cooker and not for reheating cold food.

Your machine may also have an 'Auto' setting or 'Auto cook' function. This means that the cooker will begin cooking at a higher, thermostatically controlled temperature, then automatically switch to a lower temperature. The indicator light may cycle on and off during cooking. Refer to the manufacturer's instructions for your particular model for a guide.

Choose a size of slow cooker to suit your family's needs and your kitchen work space.

Additional equipment for slow cooking

Foil straps or string pudding bowl lifter – for easier and safer removal of hot steamed puddings and other dishes from the slow cooker pot. If using foil, tear off two pieces of foil and fold each piece into three to make two long thin 'straps' of treble thickness. Lay one strap over the other at right angles to make a cross, then place the pudding basin on top where the straps meet. Lift up the ends of the straps to meet each other so that you can use them to lift the basin. Alternatively, stand the basin in a string pudding bowl lifter – a small string 'bag' with long handles available from good cookware shops or department stores.

Saucer or individual tart tin – for raising a dish off the bottom of the slow cooker pot when steaming or cooking foods in a water bath. An upturned saucer is ideal when cooking food in a large pudding basin, while an individual tart tin or large biscuit cutter makes a good base for shallower dishes or cake tins.

Heatproof mat – for protecting the table or work surface when serving food directly from the slow cooker pot.

Using your slow cooker

Because a slow cooker heats food so gently, it is the perfect way to cook meat, fish, poultry and vegetables in particular; and, since they are cooked with stocks and sauces, they stay moist and full of flavour. Because there is little evaporation, the foods do not dry out and even the cheapest cuts of meat get star treatment.

In most of the savoury recipes in this book, the ingredients are browned first in a frying pan to improve both their appearance and taste, then thickened either with flour before adding to the slow cooker pot or at the end of cooking with a little cornflour mixed to a smooth paste with cold water.

If you prefer to skip the browning stage, simply add diced, sliced or minced meat or

Save time by preparing your vegetables the night before and storing them in the refrigerator in a plastic airtight container with a little water.

chicken pieces straight from the refrigerator to the slow cooker pot, together with the vegetables cut into small dice, then cover with boiling stock. You will need to increase the cooking time, adding an extra 2–3 hours if cooking the food on 'Low'. Do not be tempted to lift the lid during the first half of cooking or you will need to add an extra 20 minutes to the cooking time.

Whether or not you brown the ingredients first, make sure that you always add hot liquid to the cooker pot.

Does the slow cooker need preheating?

The need for preheating depends on the make and model of slow cooker. Some slow cooker pots need to be preheated while empty, with the cooker set to 'High', for a minimum of 20 minutes. Others must not be heated without the addition of food. Do check the manufacturer's instructions before you begin.

How full should it be?

Make sure that the slow cooker is at least half-full for it to work efficiently or, if fuller, that there is a space of 2.5–5 cm (1–2 inches) between the brim of the cooker pot and the level of the food. Joints of meat should take up no more than two-thirds of the space. If using a pudding basin, ensure that there is 1.5 cm (¾ inch) space all the way around in a round cooker pot, or 1 cm (½ inch) at the narrowest point if using an oval-shaped slow cooker.

Getting organized

If you plan to put the slow cooker on before you go out to work in the morning, you may find it helpful to semi-prepare the dish to be cooked the night before. Chop the onion and seal it in a small plastic bag. Put diced vegetables in a plastic airtight container with a little water and then use this water to add to the cooker pot. Dice or slice meat and wrap it in clingfilm or foil.

Keep all the foods in the refrigerator, then brown them in the morning. Add boiling water to a low-salt stock cube to make hot stock or heat up the stock in the frying pan after sealing the meat. Transfer the ingredients to the slow cooker pot, then cover and leave to cook while you are out.

For the best flavour, fry onions and meat before you add them to the slow cooker pot.

Use a slow cooker to...

Make stock – put a chicken carcass in the slow cooker pot. Add a selection of vegetable trimmings, such as leek or celery tops, 2 quartered carrots and a quartered onion. Flavour with some herbs, then cover with boiling water. Cover and cook on 'Low' all day or overnight. Strain and transfer to the refrigerator or freezer as soon as it is cold.

Make a cheese fondue – add 300 g (10 oz) each grated Emmenthal and Gruyère cheese, 300 ml (½ pint) dry white wine, a little kirsch, crushed garlic, grated nutmeg and salt and pepper to a cooker pot. Cover and cook on 'Low' for 2–4 hours.

Reheat a shop-bought Christmas pudding – stand it on an upturned saucer inside the slow cooker pot and add boiling water. Cover and cook on 'High' for 3–4 hours for a 1.2 litre (2 pint) pudding or on 'Low' for 6–8 hours.

Speed up marmalade making – soften whole Seville oranges in the slow cooker with the amount of water specified in your recipe for 3–4 hours on 'High' or 6–8 hours on 'Low'. Remove from the slow cooker pot, thinly slice the oranges, then boil in a preserving pan with the cooking water and sugar.

Cooker care & cleaning

After use, make sure that your slow cooker is switched off, both on the control panel and at the electric socket outlet, and preferably keep it unplugged. Do not attempt to clean any part of the cooker until it has completely cooled down. Similarly, do not pack it away in a cupboard until completely cold. Refer to the following guidelines for cleaning your cooker, but do verify with your manufacturer's specific instructions. Ensure that the plug and electrical connections remain dry at all times.

Cooker pot and lid

Wash the slow cooker lid and ceramic pot in warm soapy water. If your lid has an air vent,

Slow cookers are easy to care for – simply wipe the cooled slow cooker base after use and remember never to immerse the base unit in water.

make sure that it is free from any tiny pieces of food. Dislodge any food stains with a washing-up brush. Some manufacturers suggest that the cooker pot may be washed in a dishwasher, but do check your instruction manual first.

For stubborn stains, fill the slow cooker pot with warm soapy water, but do not immerse the outside of the pot in water – the base is porous and will absorb water so may crack when next used in the slow cooker.

Slow cooker sense

- The outside of the slow cooker gets hot when it is switched on, so make sure that younger members of the family know not to touch it.

- Never cook food directly inside the base unit – always use the ceramic cooker pot.

- Make sure that the flex does not trail over the work surface.

- If the lid has a steam vent, make sure that the slow cooker is not sited beneath an eye-level cupboard or someone may scald themselves when reaching into the cupboard.

- Never immerse the slow cooker in water.

Slow cooker base

Wipe the outside of the cooker and buff up with a tea towel or kitchen paper. Do not use abrasive cleaner, especially if the cooker has a chrome finish. Wipe the inside of the cooker and, if it gets very dirty after prolonged use, use a little cream cleaner on a wrung-out dishcloth, then dry with kitchen paper.

Top ten tips

1 Make sure frozen food such as meat, poultry, fish and fruit is completely defrosted before adding to the slow cooker.

2 When cooking joints of meat, the size and shape is important. Keep the joint in the lower two-thirds of the cooker pot and fully cover with hot liquid. For a standard-sized slow cooker with a total capacity of 3.5 litres (6 pints) or a large 5 litre (8¾ pint) pot, do not exceed a 1 kg (2 lb) joint, although a 1.5 kg (3 lb) joint may be cooked in the larger pot provided that it is cut in half. For an extra large cooker with a total capacity of 6.5 litres (11½ pints), a 1.5 kg (3 lb) joint may be cooked whole. Always check that the joint is thoroughly cooked before serving by testing with a food thermometer or by inserting a skewer or knife through the thickest part of the joint – the juices should run clear when cooked.

3 Dried beans must be soaked overnight in cold water, then drained and rinsed and boiled vigorously in a saucepan of fresh water for 10 minutes before they can be added to the slow cooker pot.

4 Lentils do not need soaking before adding to the slow cooker.

5 When cooking rice, allow 150 ml (¼ pint) water for each 100 g (3½ oz) rice. While

Each time you remove the slow cooker lid, you will need to add an extra 10–15 minutes to the final cooking time.

basmati and ordinary white long-grain rice work well, easy-cook rice is better as it is already partially cooked with some of the starch washed off during processing, which makes it less sticky when cooked.

6 Pasta tends to go a bit soggy if added at the beginning of a recipe unless the cooking time is short. Try stirring in small pasta shapes 30–45 minutes before the end of cooking for the best results.

7 Do not add shellfish until the last 20–30 minutes of cooking. The same also applies to cream.

8 If using milk, keep to the recipe times and do not be tempted to cook the dishes for longer or you may find that the milk begins to separate. For soups or sauces, add the milk at the end of cooking if possible.

9 Root vegetables take longer to cook than meat, so dice them no larger than 1.5 cm (¾ inch) when cooking all the ingredients together and keep them submerged in the liquid to ensure even cooking.

10 All food should be covered with a liquid, gravy or sauce so that it does not dry out while cooking.

Soups & starters

Celeriac soup with Roquefort toasts

This velvety smooth soup is topped with slices of toasted French bread and Roquefort cheese. A greatly underrated vegetable, celeriac has a more delicate flavour than celery.

Serves 6

Preparation time: 30 minutes
Cooking time: 6¼–7¼ hours
Slow cooker size: standard

1 tablespoon sunflower oil
1 large onion
25 g (1 oz) butter
625 g (1¼ lb) celeriac, peeled and diced
750 ml (1¼ pints) hot vegetable or
    chicken stock
salt and pepper

To finish
300 ml (½ pint) milk
12 thin slices of French bread
100 g (3½ oz) Roquefort cheese, crumbled
150 ml (¼ pint) double cream
small bunch of chives

1 Preheat the slow cooker if necessary – see manufacturer's instructions. Heat the oil in a frying pan, add the onion and fry, stirring, for 5 minutes until softened. Add the butter and celeriac and fry for 5 more minutes.

2 Transfer the vegetables to the slow cooker pot, add the hot stock and salt and pepper and mix together. Cover with the lid and cook on 'Low' for 6–7 hours.

3 To finish the soup, ladle the celeriac mixture into a food processor or blender and blend in batches until smooth. Turn the cooker setting to 'High' and return the puréed soup to the slow cooker pot. Stir in the milk and reheat for 15 minutes.

4 Just before serving, toast the French bread on both sides under a preheated grill. Top with the cheese and return to the grill until just bubbling. Stir the cream into the soup, chop half the chives and mix into the soup, then ladle the soup into individual bowls. Float the cheese toasts on the soup and sprinkle with long pieces of chives.

Cajun red bean soup

Serves 6

Preparation time: 25 minutes, plus
* overnight soaking*
Cooking time: 8½–10½ hours
Slow cooker size: standard

125 g (4 oz) dried red kidney beans, soaked
   overnight in cold water
2 tablespoons sunflower oil
1 large onion, chopped
1 red pepper, halved, cored and diced
1 carrot, diced
1 baking potato, diced
2–3 garlic cloves, chopped (optional)
2 teaspoons mixed Cajun spice
400 g (13 oz) can chopped tomatoes
1 tablespoon soft light or dark brown sugar
1 litre (1¾ pints) hot vegetable stock
50 g (2 oz) okra, sliced
50 g (2 oz) green beans, thinly sliced
salt and pepper
crusty bread, to serve

1 Preheat the slow cooker if necessary – see
manufacturer's instructions. Drain and rinse the
soaked beans, add to a saucepan, cover with
fresh water and bring to the boil. Boil
vigorously for 10 minutes.

2 Meanwhile, heat the oil in a large frying pan.
Add the onion and fry, stirring, for 5 minutes
until softened. Add the red pepper, carrot,
potato and garlic, if using, and fry for 2–3
minutes. Stir in the mixed Cajun spice, canned

tomatoes, sugar and plenty of salt and pepper
and bring to the boil.

3 Transfer the mixture to the slow cooker pot,
add the drained beans and hot stock and mix
together. Cover with the lid and cook on 'Low'
for 8–10 hours.

4 Add the sliced green vegetables, replace the
lid and cook for 30 minutes. Ladle the soup
into bowls and serve with crusty bread.

Gingered carrot soup

Give homemade carrot soup an extra zing with ginger. Fresh root ginger has a far more intense flavour than ground ginger and can be stored for several weeks in the salad drawer of the refrigerator. This soup freezes well.

Serves 6
Preparation time: 30 minutes
Cooking time: 4¼–5¼ hours
Slow cooker size: standard

1 tablespoon sunflower oil
15 g (½ oz) butter
1 large onion, finely chopped
500 g (1 lb) carrots, diced
75 g (3 oz) red lentils
3.5 cm (1½ inch) piece of fresh root
    ginger, peeled and finely chopped
3 teaspoons mild curry paste
1.2 litres (2 pints) hot chicken or
    vegetable stock
300 ml (½ pint) full-fat milk
salt and pepper
coriander sprigs, to garnish

1 Preheat the slow cooker if necessary – see manufacturer's instructions. Heat the oil and butter in a frying pan. Add the onion and fry, stirring, for 5 minutes until pale golden.

2 Transfer the onion to the slow cooker pot and add the carrots, lentils and ginger. Mix the curry paste into the hot stock, pour into the pot and season well with salt and pepper. Stir together, then cover with the lid and cook on 'Low' for 4–5 hours.

3 The soup can be left chunky at this stage or puréed in a food processor or blender in batches until smooth. Stir in the milk, cook for 15 minutes until heated through, then ladle into individual bowls and garnish with coriander sprigs.

Salmon chowder with lime & chilli butter

Serves 6

Preparation time: 30 minutes
Cooking time: 3 hours 10 minutes–3 hours 40 minutes
Slow cooker size: standard

1 tablespoon sunflower oil
1 large onion, roughly chopped
2 potatoes, about 300 g (10 oz), finely diced
1 fennel bulb
750 ml (1¼ pints) fish stock
300 ml (½ pint) milk
300 g (10 oz) salmon fillet, skinned and halved
150 ml (¼ pint) single cream
small bunch of parsley or chives,
    roughly chopped
salt and pepper

Lime and chilli butter
½–1 large mild red chilli, halved, deseeded and
    finely chopped
75 g (3 oz) butter, at room temperature
grated rind and juice of 1 lime
pepper

1 Preheat the slow cooker if necessary – see manufacturer's instructions. Heat the oil in a frying pan, add the onion and fry, stirring, for 5 minutes until softened but not browned. Add the potatoes and cook for 3 minutes.

2 Meanwhile, cut the green feathery tops off the fennel and reserve. Cut the vegetable in half, cut away the core, then finely chop. Add the chopped fennel, stock and salt and pepper to the frying pan and bring to the boil.

3 Transfer the mixture to the slow cooker pot. Cover with the lid and cook on 'Low' for 2½–3 hours until the potato is tender. Meanwhile, make the lime and chilli butter: beat the chopped chilli into the butter with the lime rind and a little pepper. Gradually mix in the lime juice, then cover and chill well.

4 Stir the milk into the chowder, then add the salmon pieces. Replace the lid and cook for 30 minutes until the salmon flakes easily when pressed with a knife. Lift it out with a slotted spoon, put on a plate and flake into chunky pieces using a knife and fork, carefully removing any bones. Return the salmon to the soup with the cream, green fennel tops and herbs. Taste and adjust the seasoning. Replace the lid and cook for 10 minutes more.

5 Ladle the chowder into individual bowls and top with spoonfuls of the lime and chilli butter.

Cock-a-leekie soup

A traditional chicken and leek soup is given an unusual topping of oven-baked, thyme- and salt-flavoured crispy puff pastry shapes. Serve the soup with warmed bread rolls or traditional fried bread croutons instead of the pastry croutes if you prefer.

Serves 6

Preparation time: 35 minutes
Cooking time: 4¼–6¼ hours
Slow cooker size: standard

2 leeks, about 500 g (1 lb), trimmed
   and cleaned
25 g (1 oz) butter
1 tablespoon sunflower oil
4 boneless, skinless chicken thighs, diced
1 potato, about 250 g (8 oz), diced
1 litre (1¾ pints) hot chicken stock
65 g (2½ oz) pitted prunes
salt and pepper

Croutes

1 ready-rolled puff pastry sheet from a 425 g
   (14 oz) packet of 2, defrosted if frozen
1 egg, beaten
salt flakes
a few thyme sprigs

1 Preheat the slow cooker if necessary – see manufacturer's instructions. Thinly slice the leeks and separate the green slices from the white slices.

2 Heat the butter and oil in a frying pan, add the diced chicken and fry for 5 minutes, stirring until browned. Add the white leek slices and potato and fry for 2 more minutes.

3 Transfer the chicken and leek mixture to the slow cooker pot. Pour in the stock, then stir in the prunes and a little salt and pepper. Cover with the lid and cook on 'Low' for 4–6 hours.

4 When almost ready to serve, stir the reserved green leek into the soup and cook for 15 minutes. Unroll the pastry sheet and cut out 7 cm (3 inch) circles. Cut these in half, then arrange the semi-circles on a wetted baking sheet and brush with the beaten egg. Sprinkle with a few salt flakes and the torn leaves from the thyme sprigs. Bake in a preheated oven, 200°C (400°F), Gas Mark 6, for 7–8 minutes until well risen and golden.

5 Ladle the soup into individual bowls and serve topped with the pastry croutes.

Mujaddarah

Popular throughout the Arab world, this rice and lentil dish is delicious accompanied by a tossed olive and green salad. Serve larger quantities as a main dish rather than a starter if preferred and use cracked wheat (bulgar) instead of rice.

Serves 6

Preparation time: 30 minutes
Cooking time: 3½–4 hours
Slow cooker size: standard

1 tablespoon olive oil
1 large onion, chopped
1 teaspoon cumin seeds, roughly crushed
2 teaspoons coriander seeds, roughly crushed
2–3 garlic cloves, chopped
¼ teaspoon ground cinnamon
400 g (13 oz) can chopped tomatoes
2 teaspoons soft light or dark brown sugar
600 ml (1 pint) hot vegetable stock
175 g (6 oz) green lentils
100 g (3½ oz) easy-cook brown rice
salt and pepper

To serve

1 tablespoon olive oil
1 large onion, thinly sliced
small bunch of coriander or mint leaves, torn
150 ml (¼ pint) natural yogurt

1 Preheat the slow cooker if necessary – see manufacturer's instructions. Heat the oil in a large frying pan, add the chopped onion and fry, stirring, for 5 minutes until softened.

2 Stir the crushed cumin and coriander seeds into the onion with the garlic and cinnamon. Add the canned tomatoes, sugar and plenty of salt and pepper and bring to the boil, stirring.

3 Transfer the tomato mixture to the slow cooker pot, then stir in the hot stock, lentils and rice. Cover with the lid and cook on 'Low' for 3½–4 hours, stirring once or twice, until the rice and lentils are tender.

4 When almost ready to serve, heat the olive oil in a frying pan, add the sliced onion and fry for 8–10 minutes until golden brown. Spoon the lentil mixture into bowls, then top with the fried onion, torn herb leaves and spoonfuls of yogurt.

Brandied duck, walnut & green peppercorn terrine

Take this impressive pâté on a summer picnic or serve it at an alfresco weekend lunch with a bottle of red wine. It tastes lovely sliced and served with French bread, tomatoes drizzled with olive oil and garlicky marinated olives.

Serves 6

Preparation time: 45 minutes, plus
*   overnight chilling*
Cooking time: 5–6 hours
Slow cooker size: standard, large or extra large

175 g (6 oz) rashers of rindless smoked
    streaky bacon
1 tablespoon olive oil
1 onion, chopped
2 boneless spare rib pork chops, about
    275 g (9 oz)
2 boneless duck breasts, about 375 g
    (12 oz), skin and fat removed
2 garlic cloves, chopped
3 tablespoons brandy
75 g (3 oz) fresh breadcrumbs
50 g (2 oz) sun-dried tomatoes in oil, drained
    and chopped
3 pickled walnuts, drained and roughly
    chopped
1 egg, beaten
1 tablespoon green peppercorns, roughly
    crushed
salt

1 Preheat the slow cooker if necessary – see manufacturer's instructions. Lay the bacon rashers on a chopping board and stretch each one, using the flat of a large cook's knife, until half as long again. Drape the rashers across the inside of a 15 cm (6 inch) diameter, deep heatproof soufflé dish that will fit comfortably in your slow cooker pot. Press the bacon up the sides of the dish so that it is covered and leave the ends overhanging the dish.

2 Heat the oil in a frying pan, add the onion and fry, stirring, for 5 minutes until softened. Finely chop or mince the pork and 1 of the duck breasts. Cut the second duck breast into long, thin slices. Stir the garlic and chopped or minced pork and duck into the frying pan and cook for 3 minutes. Add the brandy, flame with a match and stand well back.

3 When the flames have subsided, stir in the breadcrumbs, sun-dried tomatoes, walnuts, beaten egg, peppercorns and a little salt. Mix well, then spoon half the mixture into the bacon-lined dish and press down firmly. Top with the sliced duck, then the remaining pork and walnut mixture. Fold the bacon ends over the top of the mixture, adding any leftover rashers to cover the gaps. Cover with foil.

4 Place an upturned saucer in the base of the slow cooker pot and add foil straps or a string pudding bowl lifter (see page 9), then the soufflé dish. Pour boiling water around the dish to come halfway up its sides. Cover the cooker with the lid and cook on 'High' for 5–6 hours or until the meat juices run clear when the centre of the terrine is pierced with a knife.

5 Carefully lift the terrine out of the slow cooker using the foil straps or string pudding bowl lifter and oven gloves. Stand the dish on a plate, remove the foil top and replace with greaseproof paper. Weight down the top of the terrine with measuring weights or unopened cans of food resting on top of a small plate. Transfer to the refrigerator when cool enough and chill overnight until firm.

6 Remove the weights and greaseproof paper from the terrine. Run a knife around the inside edge of the dish to loosen the terrine, then invert the dish on to a chopping board or serving plate. Jerk to release, then lift the dish off the terrine. Cut into thick slices and serve.

Tip

Black olives or prunes could be used in place of the pickled walnuts, if preferred.

Dolmades

These tiny, rice-filled vine leaf parcels will evoke holiday memories of Greece. Serve as part of a mixed mezze-style starter with bowls of taramasalata, hummus and olives.

Serves 6

Preparation time: 40 minutes, plus soaking
Cooking time: 2–2½ hours
Slow cooker size: standard – ideally oval-shaped

100 g (3½ oz) packet vacuum-packed
   vine leaves
lemon wedges, to garnish
natural Greek yogurt, to serve

Filling
100 g (3½ oz) easy-cook white rice
1 small onion, finely chopped
2 garlic cloves, crushed
40 g (1½ oz) currants
25 g (1 oz) pine nuts
3 tablespoons chopped mint or a pinch
   of dried
1 teaspoon fennel or dill seeds
2 tablespoons olive oil
finely grated rind and juice of 1 lemon
750 ml (1¼ pints) hot vegetable stock
salt and pepper

1 Remove the vine leaves from the packet and place in a bowl of cold water. Carefully loosen the leaves and transfer to a large sinkful of cold water. Leave to soak for 30 minutes. Meanwhile, preheat the slow cooker if necessary – see manufacturer's instructions.

2 Drain the vine leaves and pat dry with kitchen paper. Spread the whole undamaged leaves out on the work surface so that the stalks are towards you and the undersides are facing uppermost.

3 Mix all the filling ingredients together except the lemon juice and stock. Spoon a little of the filling on to the centre of each leaf. Fold in the sides, then loosely roll up each leaf to enclose the filling – if you roll the dolmades up too tightly, there will be no room for the rice to expand during cooking.

4 Lay any torn or badly damaged leaves in the bottom of the slow cooker pot, then arrange the vine leaf parcels in 2 or 3 layers on top. Mix the lemon juice and hot stock together and pour over the vine leaves, making sure that they are covered by the liquid. Cover with the lid and cook on 'Low' for 2–2½ hours until the rice is tender.

5 Lift the dolmades out of the slow cooker, drain well and arrange on a serving plate. Serve warm or cold, garnished with lemon wedges and accompanied by spoonfuls of Greek yogurt.

Smoked salmon timbales

Flecked with smoked salmon and basil leaves, these individual, tangy, creamy baked custards are an elegant way to start any summer dinner party. They can be made the day before if liked.

Serves 4

Preparation time: 30 minutes, plus chilling
Cooking time: 3–3½ hours
Slow cooker size: standard, large or extra large

butter, for greasing
200 ml (7 fl oz) full-fat crème fraîche
4 egg yolks
grated rind and juice of ½ lemon
1 small growing pot of basil
200 g (7 oz) sliced smoked salmon
salt and pepper
lemon wedges, to garnish (optional)

1 Preheat the slow cooker if necessary – see manufacturer's instructions. Lightly butter 4 individual 150 ml (¼ pint) metal moulds and line their bases with circles of nonstick baking or greaseproof paper.

2 Put the crème fraîche in a bowl. Gradually beat in the egg yolks, then the lemon rind and juice and season with salt and pepper. Chop half the basil and 75 g (3 oz) smoked salmon, then stir into the crème fraîche mixture.

3 Pour the mixture into the prepared moulds, then stand the moulds in the slow cooker pot – there is no need to cover them with foil. Pour hot water around the moulds to come halfway up their sides, then add the cooker lid and cook on 'Low' for 3–3½ hours or until the moulds are set.

4 Carefully remove the moulds from the slow cooker using oven gloves and leave to cool at room temperature. Transfer to the refrigerator and chill for at least 4 hours or overnight.

5 To serve, arrange the remaining smoked salmon on 4 serving plates. Loosen the edges of the timbales with a knife dipped in hot water, then invert on to the serving plates and remove the moulds. Smooth any rough areas with the side of the knife and remove the paper lining discs. Garnish with the remaining basil leaves and serve with lemon wedges, if liked.

Accompaniments

Spiced red cabbage

Gently braised red cabbage, flavoured with chillies, balsamic vinegar, honey and raisins, is delicious with grilled sausages, mackerel or a roast joint. You can replace the honey and fennel seeds with soft light brown sugar and caraway seeds if you prefer.

Serves 6

Preparation time: 15 minutes
Cooking time: 2½–3½ hours
Slow cooker size: standard

1 tablespoon olive oil
1 large onion, chopped
450 ml (¾ pint) hot vegetable or
   chicken stock
3 tablespoons balsamic vinegar
2 tablespoons thick set honey
1 tablespoon tomato purée
1 teaspoon fennel seeds, roughly crushed
½ teaspoon crushed dried chillies (optional)
625 g (1¼ lb) red cabbage, quartered, cored
   and thinly sliced
2 dessert apples, cored and diced
50 g (2 oz) raisins
salt and pepper

1 Preheat the slow cooker if necessary – see manufacturer's instructions. Heat the oil in a large frying pan, add the onion and fry, stirring, for 5 minutes until lightly browned. Stir in the stock, vinegar, honey, tomato purée and crushed fennel seeds and dried chillies, if using, then pour into the slow cooker pot.

2 Add the cabbage, apples and raisins. Season well with salt and pepper, mix together and then cover with the lid and cook on 'High' for 2½–3½ hours until the cabbage is tender.

Braised baby carrots with herb butter

Baby carrots are slowly cooked with stock, then finished with a rich green herb butter made with tarragon and chives — an easy side dish that complements roasted or grilled meats perfectly.

Serves 4–6

Preparation time: 15 minutes
Cooking time: 2–2½ hours
Slow cooker size: standard

500 g (1 lb) baby carrots, scrubbed and halved lengthways if large
250 ml (8 fl oz) hot chicken or vegetable stock
1 teaspoon thick set honey
1 tablespoon tarragon, chopped (optional)
1 tablespoon chives, chopped (optional)
salt and pepper

Herb butter
40 g (1½ oz) butter
1 tablespoon chopped tarragon
2 tablespoons chopped chives
salt and pepper

1 Preheat the slow cooker if necessary — see manufacturer's instructions. Put the carrots in the slow cooker pot with the hot stock, honey, herbs and salt and pepper. Cover with the lid and cook on 'High' for 2–2½ hours until tender.

2 Meanwhile, beat the butter with the herbs and a little salt and pepper. Chill until required. Drain and transfer the carrots to a serving dish, dot the herb butter over the top and serve.

Cheesy vegetable galette

Transform everyday vegetables by flavouring them with garlic and bathing them in a rich cheesy sauce, ready to serve with grilled chops or fish.

Serves 4–5

Preparation time: 25 minutes

Cooking time: 3–4 hours

Slow cooker size: standard

50 g (2 oz) butter, plus extra for greasing

50 g (2 oz) plain flour

600 ml (1 pint) full-fat milk

2–3 garlic cloves, finely chopped

100 g (3½ oz) strong Cheddar cheese, grated

625 g (1¼ lb) small baking potatoes, thinly sliced

1 carrot, thinly sliced

1 parsnip, thinly sliced

½ large onion, finely chopped

salt and pepper

chopped parsley, to garnish (optional)

1 Preheat the slow cooker if necessary – see manufacturer's instructions. Melt the butter in a saucepan, stir in the flour and cook for 1 minute. Gradually stir in the milk and bring to the boil, stirring continuously until thickened and smooth. Stir in the garlic, three-quarters of the cheese and a little salt and pepper.

2 Brush the inside of the slow cooker pot with a little butter, then layer half the root vegetables and onion in the pot. Cover with half the cheese sauce, then continue layering the vegetables. Pour the remaining hot cheese sauce over the top and sprinkle with the remaining cheese.

3 Cover the cooker with the lid and cook on 'Low' for 3–4 hours until the vegetables are tender. Sprinkle with a little chopped parsley, if liked, and serve.

Tip

While most dishes made in a slow cooker are fine if left to cook longer than the time stated, those made with milk are the exception and must be served within the time specified in the recipe.

Saffron-baked potatoes

Give plain boiled potatoes a lift by cooking them slowly with saffron, garlic and North African spices. Serve with barbecued or grilled meats or with fish steaks.

Serves 6

Preparation time: 15 minutes
Cooking time: 4–5 hours
Slow cooker size: standard

2 tablespoons olive oil
1 large onion, thinly sliced
1 teaspoon cumin seeds, roughly crushed
1 teaspoon coriander seeds, roughly crushed
large pinch of saffron threads
½ teaspoon turmeric
2 garlic cloves, chopped
450 ml (¾ pint) chicken or vegetable stock
50 g (2 oz) sultanas
½ teaspoon salt
1 kg (2 lb) new potatoes, scrubbed and
    cut into pieces no larger than 3.5 cm
    (1½ inches) square
pepper
chopped coriander leaves, to garnish (optional)

1 Preheat the slow cooker if necessary – see manufacturer's instructions. Heat the oil in a frying pan, add the onion and fry, stirring, for 5 minutes until lightly browned.

2 Stir the crushed cumin and coriander seeds into the onion with the saffron, turmeric and garlic and cook for 1 minute. Pour in the stock, then add the sultanas, salt and a little pepper. Bring to the boil, stirring.

3 Pour the onion mixture into the slow cooker pot. Add the potato chunks, making sure they are below the level of the liquid. Cover with the lid and cook on 'Low' for 4–5 hours until tender. Transfer to a serving dish and sprinkle with chopped coriander, if liked.

Tip

Try to cut the potatoes to as similar a size as possible so that they cook evenly – the larger they are, the longer they will take to cook. Old baking potatoes may also be used.

Tamarind lentils & vegetables

Popular in southern India, this red lentil-based dish is flavoured with root ginger, turmeric and tamarind paste, and finished with fresh coriander. Serve it with rice and meaty curries.

Serves 6

Preparation time: 20 minutes
Cooking time: 7–8 hours
Slow cooker size: standard

1 tablespoon sunflower oil
1 large onion, chopped
3.5 cm (1½ inch) piece of fresh root
    ginger, peeled and finely chopped
2–3 garlic cloves, chopped
1 teaspoon turmeric
½ teaspoon crushed dried chillies
2 teaspoons soft light brown sugar
2 teaspoons tamarind paste
900 ml (1½ pints) vegetable stock
175 g (6 oz) red lentils
1 potato, about 250 g (8 oz), diced
2 carrots, diced
small bunch of coriander
salt and pepper

1 Preheat the slow cooker if necessary – see manufacturer's instructions. Heat the oil in a frying pan, add the onion and fry, stirring, for 5 minutes until lightly browned.

2 Stir in the ginger, garlic, turmeric and crushed dried chillies, then add the sugar, tamarind paste and stock. Season with salt and pepper and bring to the boil, stirring.

3 Pour the mixture into the slow cooker pot. Stir in the red lentils and diced vegetables. Cover with the lid and cook for 7–8 hours until the lentils are tender. Finely chop about 4 tablespoons of the coriander, stir into the lentils, then garnish with the remaining leaves.

Tips

Derived from a fruit known as the Indian date, tamarind paste is sold in jars and found in the dry spices section of good supermarkets.

Top the lentils with halved dried chillies and a few curry leaves warmed in a little extra oil or with a little finely chopped fresh red chilli, if liked.

Coconut & lime rice

Cooking several different dishes at once is easy if you leave the rice to cook unattended in the slow cooker. Adding the lime rind and juice at the end of cooking accounts for the intensity of the flavour. Thai rice is a little stickier than basmati rice.

Serves 4

Preparation time: 5 minutes
Cooking time: 1¼–1½ hours
Slow cooker size: standard, large or extra large

250 g (8 oz) Thai fragrant rice
25 g (1 oz) wild rice
40 g (1½ oz) creamed coconut
600 ml (1 pint) boiling water
grated rind and juice of 2 limes
salt

1 Preheat the slow cooker if necessary – see manufacturer's instructions. Put the Thai and wild rice in a sieve and rinse well under cold running water. Find a large heatproof bowl that will fit comfortably in your slow cooker pot, add the creamed coconut and mix to a paste with a little of the boiling water. Stir in the rest of the boiling water, rinsed rice and salt.

2 Cover the bowl with foil, then stand it in the slow cooker pot on top of an upturned saucer. Pour boiling water to come halfway up the sides of the bowl, then cover the cooker with its lid. Cook on 'High' for 1¼–1½ hours or until the rice is tender.

3 Fluff the rice up with a fork, draining off any excess liquid. Stir in the lime rind and juice and a little extra boiling water if needed, then serve.

Meat, poultry & game

Malaysian beef & aubergine curry

Quick and easy to put together, this spicy curry tastes delicious topped with pak choi stir-fried with a little ginger, and accompanied by plain rice.

Serves 4

Preparation time: 25 minutes
Cooking time: 8–9 hours
Slow cooker size: standard

1 large onion
3–4 garlic cloves
2 tablespoons sunflower oil
500 g (1 lb) diced braising beef
1 large aubergine, cut into chunks
2 tablespoons red Thai curry paste
1 tablespoon fish sauce
400 ml (14 fl oz) can coconut milk
boiled rice, to serve

1 Preheat the slow cooker if necessary – see manufacturer's instructions. Process in a food processor or very finely chop the onion and garlic until almost paste-like. Heat the oil in a frying pan, add the onion and garlic and fry, stirring, for 2–3 minutes until softened.

2 Add the beef and aubergine, a few pieces at a time, and fry until browned. Stir in the curry paste, fish sauce and coconut milk. Bring to the boil, then transfer to the slow cooker pot.

3 Cover with the lid and cook on 'Low' for 8–9 hours until the meat is tender. Serve with plain boiled rice.

Tip

If you prefer to use creamed coconut rather than canned coconut milk, cook the beef in 400 ml (14 fl oz) chicken stock and crumble in 50 g (2 oz) creamed coconut at the end of cooking.

Beef & ale hotpot

This full-bodied traditional hotpot topped with thinly sliced potatoes also has a surprise layer of sliced celeriac, which adds a delicious and subtle celery flavour to this dish. Baby carrots make an ideal accompaniment.

Tip

If the slow cooker pot fits under your grill, you may like to brown the top of the potatoes before serving.

Serves 6

Preparation time: 30 minutes
Cooking time: 5–6 hours
Slow cooker size: large or extra large

2 tablespoons sunflower oil
1 kg (2 lb) braising beef, trimmed of fat
  and cubed
1 large onion, chopped
3 tablespoons plain flour
500 ml (17 fl oz) can brown ale, stout
  or barley wine
4 teaspoons wholegrain mustard
3 teaspoons soft light or dark brown sugar
2 tablespoons tomato purée
450 ml (¾ pint) hot beef stock
425 g (14 oz) celeriac, peeled and thinly sliced
625 g (1¼ lb) similarly sized baking potatoes,
  thinly sliced
25 g (1 oz) butter, melted
salt and pepper
finely chopped chives, to garnish (optional)

1 Preheat the slow cooker if necessary – see manufacturer's instructions. Heat half of the oil in a large frying pan, gradually add half the beef and fry over a high heat, stirring until browned. Remove the beef from the pan with a slotted spoon and transfer to a plate.

2 Heat the remaining oil in the pan, add the remaining beef and the onion and fry over a high heat, stirring, until browned. Stir in the flour, then add the beer, mustard, sugar, tomato purée and plenty of salt and pepper. Bring to the boil, stirring, then transfer to the slow cooker pot with the reserved fried beef. Stir in the hot stock.

3 Arrange the celeriac slices overlapping each other on top of the beef, then cover with the sliced potatoes. Brush with the melted butter, sprinkle with a little extra salt and pepper, then cover the cooker with the lid and cook on 'High' for 5–6 hours. Garnish with a sprinkling of finely chopped chives, if liked, to finish.

Steak & mushroom pudding

A slow cooker really comes into its own when steaming puddings. Forget about kitchen windows running with condensation or saucepans boiling dry – simply place the pudding in the slow cooker, switch it on and leave.

Serves 4

Preparation time: 40 minutes
Cooking time: 5–6 hours
Slow cooker size: standard, large or extra large

25 g (1 oz) butter, plus extra for greasing
1 tablespoon sunflower oil
2 large onions, roughly chopped
2 teaspoons caster sugar
100 g (3½ oz) cup mushrooms, sliced
1 tablespoon plain or self-raising flour
150 ml (¼ pint) hot beef stock
1 teaspoon Dijon mustard
1 tablespoon Worcestershire sauce
700 g (1 lb 6 oz) rump steak, trimmed of fat
   and thinly sliced
salt and pepper
buttered cabbage and mashed swede, to serve

Pastry

300 g (10 oz) self-raising flour, plus
   extra for dusting
½ teaspoon salt
150 g (5 oz) shredded suet
200 ml (7 fl oz) water

1 Preheat the slow cooker if necessary – see manufacturer's instructions. Heat the butter and oil in a frying pan, add the onions and fry for 5 minutes until softened. Sprinkle the sugar over the onions and fry for 5 more minutes until browned. Add the mushrooms and fry for 2–3 minutes, then stir in the flour.

2 Mix together the stock, mustard, Worcestershire sauce and salt and pepper in a jug.

3 To make the pastry, put the flour, salt and suet in a bowl and mix well. Gradually stir in the water to make a soft but not sticky dough. Knead the dough lightly, then roll out on a floured surface to a circle 33 cm (13 inches) in diameter. Cut a quarter segment out of the circle and reserve for the lid.

4 Butter a 1.5 litre (2½ pint) pudding basin that will fit comfortably in your slow cooker pot with a space of at least 1.5 cm (¾ inch) all the way around. Lift the remaining pastry into the basin. Bring the cut edges together, overlapping them slightly so that the basin is completely lined with pastry, and press them together to seal.

5 Fill the pastry-lined pudding basin with alternate layers of fried onion and mushrooms and sliced steak. Pour the hot stock mixture over the top. Pat the reserved piece of pastry into a round the same size as the top of the basin. Fold the top edges of the pastry in the

basin over the meat filling, brush with a little water, then cover with the pastry lid.

6 Cover the pudding with a large circle of buttered and pleated foil or dome the foil 'lid' slightly so that there is room for the pastry to rise. Tie the foil in place with a length of string tied around the basin, under the rim, and add a string handle. Stand the basin in the slow cooker pot on top of an upturned saucer. Pour boiling water into the slow cooker pot to come halfway up the side of the pudding basin.

7 Add the lid and cook the pudding on 'High' for 5–6 hours. Remove the basin from the slow cooker, then remove the string and foil – the pastry should have risen and feel dry to the touch. Serve the pudding with buttered cabbage and mashed swede.

Burgundy beef stew with horseradish dumplings

This homely stew topped with light and fluffy horseradish-flavoured, chive-speckled dumplings is just the thing to restore flagging spirits after a long hectic day, and requires no accompaniments. Simply spoon into shallow dishes and enjoy.

Serves 4

Preparation time: 35 minutes
Cooking time: 8–10 1/2 hours
Slow cooker size: standard

2 tablespoons olive oil
750 g (1 1/2 lb) braising beef, trimmed of fat
   and cubed
1 large onion, chopped
2–3 garlic cloves, chopped
2 tablespoons plain flour
300 ml (1/2 pint) Burgundy red wine
300 ml (1/2 pint) beef stock
1 tablespoon tomato purée
2 bay leaves
150 g (5 oz) baby carrots, scrubbed and halved
   legthways if too large
250 g (8 oz) leeks, trimmed, cleaned and
   thinly sliced
salt and pepper

Horseradish dumplings
150 g (5 oz) self-raising flour
75 g (3 oz) shredded suet
2 teaspoons creamed horseradish
3 tablespoons chopped chives
5–7 tablespoons water
salt and pepper

1 Preheat the slow cooker if necessary – see manufacturer's instructions. Heat the oil in a frying pan and add the beef, a few cubes at a time, until all the pieces have been added to the pan. Fry over a high heat until just beginning to brown, then add the onion and fry, stirring, for 5 minutes.

2 Stir in the garlic and flour, then gradually mix in the wine and stock. Add the tomato purée and bay leaves and season with salt and

Tip

Beer can be used instead of the red wine, if preferred. If using a very strong beer such as barley wine or dry stout, use only 200 ml (7 fl oz) and make up to 300 ml (1/2 pint) with extra beef stock.

pepper. Bring to the boil, then transfer the mixture to the slow cooker pot. Cover with the lid and cook on 'Low' for 7–9 hours.

3 Stir the stew, then add the carrots and cook on 'High' for 30–45 minutes. Meanwhile, make the dumplings: mix the flour, suet, horseradish, chives and salt and pepper in a bowl. Stir in enough water to make a soft but not sticky dough. With floured hands, shape into 8 balls.

4 Stir the leeks into the stew, then add the dumplings, replace the lid and cook for another 30–45 minutes until the dumplings are light and fluffy. Spoon into shallow dishes and serve, remembering to remove the bay leaves.

Braised oxtail with port

Serves 4

Preparation time: 25 minutes
Cooking time: 9–10 hours
Slow cooker size: standard

1 tablespoon sunflower oil
1 well-trimmed oxtail, about 1 kg (2 lb),
   thickly sliced
1 large onion, chopped
2 tablespoons plain flour
250 ml (8 fl oz) ruby port
450 ml (¾ pint) beef stock
1 cinnamon stick, halved
1 teaspoon ground mace
2 teaspoons juniper berries, roughly crushed
2 tablespoons tomato purée
1 red pepper, halved, cored and deseeded
oil, for brushing
salt and pepper
1 portion of cannellini bean mash (see Tip)

1 Preheat the slow cooker if necessary – see manufacturer's instructions. Heat the oil in a frying pan, add the oxtail and fry, in batches if necessary, until browned. Lift out and place on a plate.

2 Add the onion to the pan and fry until pale golden. Stir in the flour, then add the port, stock, cinnamon stick, mace, juniper berries and tomato purée and season with salt and pepper. Bring to the boil, stirring.

Tip

To make cannellini bean mash, drain 2 x 410 g (13½ oz) cans of cannellini beans and rinse the beans. Mash or process them with a little milk or double cream, then flavour with finely chopped and lightly fried onion and seasoning. Warm through in a saucepan.

3 Transfer the oxtail to the slow cooker pot, then pour in the hot stock mixture, making sure that the oxtail is completely covered. Add the lid and cook on 'Low' for 9–10 hours. Just before serving, put the red pepper halves, skin side uppermost, on a piece of foil in a grill pan. Brush with oil and grill until the skin is blackened. Cool for 10 minutes, then peel off the skin and cut the pepper into thin slices.

4 Spoon the oxtail and sauce into shallow dishes, discarding the cinnamon stick. Garnish with the grilled sliced red pepper and serve with cannellini bean mash. Provide a separate bowl for the bones or remove them before serving – the meat is so tender after such long cooking, it almost falls off the bone.

Mince & macaroni

This is a good midweek supper standby, based on minced beef or lamb, a can of tomatoes and dried macaroni. You can replace 150 ml (¼ pint) of the stock with red wine if liked.

Serves 4

Preparation time: 20 minutes, plus soaking
Cooking time: 8–9 hours
Slow cooker size: standard

15 g (½ oz) mixed dried mushrooms
150 ml (¼ pint) boiling water
1 tablespoon olive oil
500 g (1 lb) minced beef or lamb
1 large onion, chopped
2 garlic cloves, chopped
400 g (13 oz) can chopped tomatoes
450 ml (¾ pint) chicken stock
2 tablespoons tomato purée
¼ teaspoon grated nutmeg
small bunch of rosemary
250 g (8 oz) macaroni
3 tablespoons pine nuts, toasted
salt and pepper

1 Preheat the slow cooker if necessary – see manufacturer's instructions. Put the mushrooms in a heatproof bowl, pour over the boiling water and leave to soak for 20 minutes.

2 Meanwhile, heat the oil in a frying pan. Add the minced meat and onion and fry, stirring, for 5 minutes until browned. Add the garlic, then stir in the canned tomatoes, stock, tomato purée and nutmeg. Tear the leaves off 3 of the rosemary sprigs and add to the mince with the reconstituted dried mushrooms and their soaking liquid, and salt and pepper.

3 Transfer the mixture to the slow cooker pot, cover with the lid and cook on 'Low' for 8–9 hours. When ready to serve, cook the macaroni in a saucepan of boiling water until tender. Drain and mix into the cooked mince. Spoon on to individual plates and top with the toasted pine nuts and rosemary leaves, stripped from the remaining sprigs.

Tip

To make in a larger slow cooker, increase the ingredient quantities by half as much again and cook for the same length of time.

Spiced lamb tagine

Serves 6–8

Preparation time: 35 minutes
Cooking time: 8½–10½ hours
Slow cooker size: large or extra large

1 tablespoon olive oil
500 g (1 lb) minced lamb
1 large onion, chopped
2–3 garlic cloves, chopped
3.5 cm (1½ inch) piece of fresh root ginger,
    peeled and finely chopped
1 teaspoon turmeric
1 teaspoon ground cinnamon
½ teaspoon ground allspice
2 tablespoons plain flour
400 g (13 oz) can chopped tomatoes
750 ml (1¼ pints) lamb or chicken stock
1 tablespoon tomato purée
300 g (10 oz) new potatoes, scrubbed and
    halved or quartered, depending on size
300 g (10 oz) butternut squash, deseeded,
    peeled and diced
2 carrots, diced
50 g (2 oz) raisins
300 g (10 oz) frozen broad beans
150 g (5 oz) frozen peas
small bunch of mint, leaves torn
salt and pepper
couscous, to serve

1 Preheat the slow cooker if necessary – see manufacturer's instructions. Heat the oil in a large frying pan. Add the mince and onion and fry, stirring, for 5 minutes until the mince is browned. Stir in the garlic, ginger, spices and flour, then add the canned tomatoes, stock and tomato purée.

2 Mix in the potatoes, butternut squash, carrots and raisins, then season with salt and pepper. Bring to the boil, then transfer to the slow cooker pot. Cover with the lid and cook on 'Low' for 8–10 hours.

3 Stir the tagine, then sprinkle the frozen vegetables over the top. Replace the lid and cook for another 20–30 minutes until the vegetables are hot. Spoon on to individual plates, sprinkle with the torn mint leaves and serve with couscous.

Greek-style lamb shanks

Long, slow cooking brings out the natural sweetness of the lamb, which is complemented by the delicate lemon flavour of the crushed coriander seeds and bay leaves. Sliced lamb shoulder or leg steaks can also be cooked in this way.

Serves 4

Preparation time: 20 minutes
Cooking time: 5–7 hours
Slow cooker size: standard

1 tablespoon olive oil
4 lamb shanks, about 1.5 kg (3 lb)
1 large onion, thinly sliced
4 teaspoons coriander seeds, roughly crushed
2 tablespoons plain flour
600 ml (1 pint) chicken or lamb stock
150 ml (¼ pint) dry sherry, dry cider or white wine
4 bay leaves
2 teaspoons clear honey
salt and pepper
mashed potatoes or rice and a green salad with black olives, to serve

To garnish
oregano leaves
grated lemon rind

1 Preheat the slow cooker if necessary – see manufacturer's instructions. Heat the oil in a frying pan, add the lamb shanks and brown on all sides. Transfer them to the slow cooker pot, arranging them so that they almost stand up with the thickest parts on the bottom of the pot.

2 Add the onion to the frying pan and fry, stirring, for 5 minutes until lightly browned. Add the crushed coriander seeds and cook for 1 minute. Stir in the flour, then add the stock, sherry, cider or wine, bay leaves and honey and season with salt and pepper. Bring to the boil, then pour over the lamb. Cover with the lid and cook on 'High' for 5–7 hours until the meat almost falls off the bone. (The 'High' setting is necessary because the shanks are much denser than cubed meat.) Turn the meat once during cooking, if possible.

3 Transfer the lamb shanks to a serving bowl, cover and keep hot. Carefully lift the slow cooker pot out of the base unit using oven gloves, pour the contents into a saucepan and boil rapidly to reduce the liquid by half. (Alternatively, simply thicken the liquid with a little cornflour mixed to a smooth paste with cold water instead.) Spoon the sauce and onions over the lamb, discarding the bay leaves, then garnish with oregano leaves and lemon rind. Serve with creamy mashed potatoes, or with rice and a green salad mixed with black olives.

Lamb daube

This classic French-style lamb stew slowly cooked with red wine and finished with shallots and bacon is delicious served with mashed celeriac or potatoes and green beans. The prunes add a marvellous flavour to the gravy.

Serves 4

Preparation time: 30 minutes
Cooking time: 7½–8½ hours
Slow cooker size: standard

2 tablespoons olive oil
700 g (1 lb 6 oz) lean lamb, diced
1 large onion, chopped
50 g (2 oz) streaky bacon, rinded and diced
2 garlic cloves, chopped
1 tablespoon plain flour
200 ml (7 fl oz) red wine
300 ml (½ pint) lamb or chicken stock
1 tablespoon tomato purée
75 g (3 oz) pitted prunes (optional)
fresh or dried bouquet garni
salt and pepper

To finish

15 g (½ oz) butter
1 tablespoon olive oil
175 g (6 oz) shallots, halved if large
50 g (2 oz) streaky bacon, rinded and diced

1 Preheat the slow cooker if necessary – see manufacturer's instructions. Heat the oil in a frying pan, then add the lamb, a few pieces at a time, until it has all been added to the pan. Cook over a high heat until browned. Drain and transfer to a plate.

2 Add the onion and bacon to the pan and fry for 5 minutes until pale golden. Add the garlic, then stir in the flour. Add the wine, stock, tomato purée, prunes, if using, and bouquet garni and season with salt and pepper. Bring to the boil, stirring.

3 Transfer the mixture to the slow cooker pot, add the lamb and mix together. Cover with the lid and cook on 'Low' for 7–8 hours. To finish, heat the butter and oil in the cleaned frying pan, add the shallots and bacon and fry until golden. Stir into the lamb casserole and cook for 30 minutes, then serve.

Tips

To make in a larger slow cooker, increase the ingredient quantities by half as much again and cook for the same length of time.

Use braising beef in place of the lamb if preferred.

Peppered pork pot

This Italian-inspired casserole is delicious served with mashed potatoes or creamy soft polenta.

Serves 4

Preparation time: 25 minutes
Cooking time: 8–10 hours
Slow cooker size: standard

1 tablespoon olive oil
4 boneless spare rib pork chops, about 700 g
    (1 lb 6 oz)
1 onion, chopped
1 red pepper, halved, cored, deseeded
    and sliced
1 orange or yellow pepper, halved, cored
    deseeded and sliced
2 garlic cloves, chopped
2 tablespoons plain flour
400 g (13 oz) can chopped tomatoes
200 ml (7 fl oz) chicken stock
a few thyme sprigs
salt and pepper
mashed potatoes or polenta, to serve

1 Preheat the slow cooker if necessary – see manufacturer's instructions. Heat the oil in a frying pan, add the pork chops and brown on both sides. Remove and transfer to a plate.

2 Add the onion to the pan and fry, stirring, for 5 minutes until lightly browned. Stir in the peppers and garlic and fry for 1 minute. Stir in the flour, then add the canned tomatoes, stock and thyme and season with salt and pepper. Bring to the boil, stirring.

3 Transfer the pork chops to the slow cooker pot and cover with the tomato mixture. Add the lid, then cook on 'Low' for 8–10 hours. Spoon on to plates and serve on a bed of mashed potatoes or polenta.

Hungarian goulash

Goulash is often considered a mild stew, although a true Hungarian goulash can be quite fiery since the paprika available in Eastern Europe comes in four strengths. Combine paprika with chilli powder for a hotter version of this dish. Serve with warmed sauerkraut or plain boiled potatoes.

Serves 4

Preparation time: 25 minutes
Cooking time: 8–10 hours
Slow cooker size: standard

1 tablespoon sunflower oil
700 g (1 lb 6 oz) pork, diced
1 large onion, chopped
150 g (5 oz) button mushrooms, halved
2 teaspoons paprika, plus extra to garnish
¼ teaspoon ground cinnamon
¼ teaspoon ground allspice
1 teaspoon caraway seeds
2 tablespoons plain flour
400 g (13 oz) can chopped tomatoes
450 ml (¾ pint) hot chicken stock
salt and pepper
soured cream, to serve

1 Preheat the slow cooker if necessary – see manufacturer's instructions. Heat the oil in a frying pan, then add the pork, a few pieces at a time, until it has all been added to the pan. Stir in the onion and cook for 5 minutes until lightly browned.

2 Add the mushrooms and cook for 2 minutes. Stir in the spices and the flour and cook for 1 minute. Mix in the canned tomatoes, then bring the mixture to the boil.

3 Transfer the mixture to the slow cooker pot. Stir in the stock and season with salt and pepper, cover with the lid and cook on 'Low' for 8–10 hours.

4 Spoon the goulash on to plates, top with spoonfuls of soured cream and sprinkle with a little extra paprika, to garnish.

Pot-roasted chicken with lemon

A whole chicken can be very successfully cooked in a slow cooker. By starting the bird breast side down, the breast stays moister and won't come to any harm if the dinner gets delayed.

Serves 4–5

Preparation time: 25 minutes
Cooking time: 5–6 hours
Slow cooker size: large or extra large

1.5 kg (3 lb) whole chicken
2 tablespoons olive oil
1 large onion, cut into 6 wedges
500 ml (17 fl oz) dry cider
3 teaspoons Dijon mustard
2 teaspoons caster sugar
900 ml (1½ pints) hot chicken stock
3 carrots, cut into chunky pieces
3 celery sticks, thickly sliced
1 lemon, cut into 6 wedges
20 g (¾ oz) tarragon
3 tablespoons crème fraîche
salt and pepper
lemon wedges, to garnish (optional)

1 Preheat the slow cooker if necessary – see manufacturer's instructions. Wash the chicken inside and out with cold water, then pat dry with kitchen paper. Heat the oil in a large frying pan, add the chicken, breast side down, and fry for 10 minutes, turning the chicken several times until browned all over.

2 Carefully put the chicken, breast side down, in the slow cooker pot. Fry the onion wedges in the remaining oil in the pan until lightly browned. Add the cider, mustard and sugar, season with salt and pepper and bring to the boil. Pour over the chicken, add the hot stock, then add the vegetables, lemon wedges and 3 sprigs of the tarragon, making sure that the chicken and all the vegetables are well below the level of the stock so that they cook evenly and thoroughly.

3 Cover with the cooker lid and cook the chicken on 'High' for 5–6 hours until it is thoroughly cooked and the meat juices run clear when the thickest parts of the leg and breast are pierced with a sharp knife. Turn the chicken after 4 hours, if liked.

4 Lift the chicken out of the stock, drain well and transfer to a large serving plate. Remove the vegetables using a slotted spoon and arrange them around the chicken. Measure 600 ml (1 pint) of the hot cooking stock from the slow cooker pot into a jug. Reserve a few sprigs of tarragon to garnish, chop the remainder and whisk into the stock with the crème fraîche to make a gravy. Adjust the seasoning to taste. Carve the chicken in the usual way and serve with the gravy and vegetables. Garnish with fresh lemon wedges, if liked, and the reserved tarragon sprigs.

Spanish chicken pot

Spicy chorizo adds an authentic Mediterranean flavour to an everyday chicken casserole. Buy the sausage whole from the delicatessen counter and dice it yourself as it has much more flavour than packets of wafer-thin ready-sliced chorizo.

Serves 6–8

Preparation time: 30 minutes
Cooking time: 8–10 hours
Slow cooker size: large or extra large

2 tablespoons olive oil
6 chicken thighs, skinned if liked
6 chicken drumsticks, skinned if liked
1 large slice of onion
2–3 garlic cloves, chopped
3 tablespoons plain flour
2 x 400 g (13 oz) cans chopped tomatoes
150 g (5 oz) piece of chorizo sausage, diced
750 g (1½ lb) baby new potatoes, scrubbed
    and halved or quartered, depending on size
450 ml (¾ pint) hot chicken stock
65 g (2½ oz) pitted black olives
a few rosemary sprigs or a pinch of dried
salt and pepper
basil or extra rosemary sprigs, to garnish
crusty bread, to serve

1 Preheat the slow cooker if necessary – see manufacturer's instructions. Heat the oil in a large frying pan and fry the chicken in batches until browned on all sides. Drain and transfer to a large plate.

2 Add the onion to the pan and fry for 5 minutes until pale golden. Stir in the garlic, then the flour. Add the canned tomatoes and chorizo and season with salt and pepper. Bring to the boil.

3 Transfer the chicken and potatoes to the slow cooker pot, pour in the tomato mixture, then add the hot stock, olives and rosemary. Cover with the lid and cook on 'Low' for 8–10 hours until the chicken is tender.

4 Spoon into shallow dishes, sprinkle with basil or rosemary sprigs and serve with plenty of warmed crusty bread to dunk into the delicious sauce.

Persian chicken

This wonderfully vibrant golden-coloured casserole has a mellow spiced flavour and makes an easy supper dish served on a bed of couscous mixed with dried fruits.

Serves 4

Preparation time: 30 minutes
Cooking time: 8¼–9¼ hours
Slow cooker size: standard

4 chicken drumsticks, skinned
4 chicken thighs, skinned
2 tablespoons plain flour
I teaspoon turmeric
I teaspoon paprika
2 tablespoons olive oil
I large onion, chopped
2 garlic cloves, chopped (optional)
4 cloves
2.5 cm (I inch) piece of fresh root ginger, finely chopped
450 ml (¾ pint) chicken stock
125 g (4 oz) young spinach, well washed, larger leaves torn into pieces
salt and pepper
couscous, to serve

1 Preheat the slow cooker if necessary – see manufacturer's instructions. Slash each piece of chicken 2 or 3 times with a small, sharp knife. Mix the flour, turmeric and paprika on a plate, then use to thinly coat the chicken.

2 Heat the oil in a frying pan, add the chicken and cook until browned on all sides. Transfer to a plate. Add the onion and garlic, if using, to the pan and fry, stirring, for 5 minutes until lightly browned.

3 Stir in any remaining spiced flour. Add the cloves, ginger, stock and salt and pepper to taste and bring to the boil, stirring.

4 Pack the chicken joints into the slow cooker pot, then pour in the hot stock mixture. Cover with the lid and cook for 8–9 hours until the chicken is tender. Add the spinach and cook for 15 minutes more, then serve the chicken on a bed of couscous.

Sun-dried tomato & chicken pilaf

Whole chicken breasts are flavoured with a rich sun-dried tomato sauce and braised on a base of wild and basmati rice. Serve with rocket leaves tossed in an olive oil and lemon dressing for an easy supper.

Tip

The dish will not come to any harm if left to cook for longer than the time specified, although you will need to top up the pot with a little extra hot chicken stock.

Serves 4

Preparation time: 25 minutes
Cooking time: 2½–3 hours
Slow cooker size: standard

1 tablespoon olive oil
4 boneless, skinless chicken breasts
1 large onion, roughly chopped
2 garlic cloves, chopped (optional)
400 g (13 oz) can chopped tomatoes
50 g (2 oz) sun-dried tomatoes in oil, drained
    and sliced
2 teaspoons pesto
600 ml (1 pint) hot chicken stock
150 g (5 oz) basmati rice
50 g (2 oz) wild rice
salt and pepper
rocket salad, to serve

1 Preheat the slow cooker if necessary – see manufacturer's instructions. Heat the oil in a frying pan, then fry the chicken breasts on one side only until browned. Remove from the pan with a slotted spoon and reserve on a plate.

2 Fry the onion and garlic, if using, in the pan for 5 minutes, stirring, until lightly browned. Add the canned tomatoes, sun-dried tomatoes and pesto, season with salt and pepper and bring to the boil. Pour into the slow cooker pot, then stir in the hot stock.

3 Rinse the basmati rice well in a sieve under cold running water, then stir into the slow cooker pot with the wild rice. Arrange the chicken breasts on top of the rice, browned side uppermost, pressing them just below the level of the liquid so that they don't dry out during cooking. Cover with the lid and cook on 'High' for 2½–3 hours until the chicken is thoroughly cooked and the rice is tender.

4 Spoon on to serving plates and serve with a rocket salad.

Turkey chilli with chocolate

Mexican cooks have long used dark chocolate in savoury dishes – it combines unusually well with chicken or turkey, and with chilli. Serve with tortillas or rice and a side salad.

Serves 4
Preparation time: 25 minutes
Cooking time: 8–10 hours
Slow cooker size: standard

1 tablespoon sunflower oil
500 g (1 lb) minced turkey
1 large onion, chopped
2 garlic cloves, chopped
½–1 teaspoon chilli powder
1 teaspoon cumin seeds, roughly crushed
½ teaspoon ground cinnamon
¼ teaspoon ground cloves
1 tablespoon plain flour
410 g (13½ oz) can red kidney beans, drained and rinsed
400 g (13 oz) can chopped tomatoes
450 ml (¾ pint) chicken stock
1 tablespoon tomato purée
25 g (1 oz) dark chocolate, chopped
salt and pepper

To serve
4 soft tortillas
guacamole (see Tip)
4 tablespoons soured cream

1 Preheat the slow cooker if necessary – see manufacturer's instructions. Heat the oil in a frying pan, add the minced turkey and onion and fry, stirring, for 5 minutes until browned. Stir in the garlic, spices and flour, then add the kidney beans, canned tomatoes, stock, tomato purée and chocolate and season with salt and pepper.

2 Bring to the boil, breaking up any large pieces of mince, then transfer the mixture to the slow cooker pot. Cover with the lid and cook on 'Low' for 8–10 hours. Stir well and serve in warmed soft tortillas topped with guacamole and spoonfuls of soured cream.

Tips

If you have an extra large slow cooker, simply double the ingredient quantities and cook for the same length of time.

To make guacamole, halve an avocado and remove the stone, scoop out the flesh with a spoon, then mash with fresh lime or lemon juice and season with salt and pepper.

Venison sausage & lentil stew

Unlike most dried pulses, lentils do not require soaking before use. They are partnered here with cranberries and meaty venison sausages to make a tasty sausage casserole. Use Toulouse or other coarse pork sausages instead of venison if preferred.

Serves 4

Preparation time: 20 minutes
Cooking time: 6–7 hours
Slow cooker size: standard

1 tablespoon olive oil

8 venison sausages

1 large onion, chopped

2 garlic cloves, chopped (optional)

2 tablespoons plain flour

900 ml (1½ pints) chicken stock

3 tablespoons soft light or dark brown sugar

2 tablespoons tomato purée

2 tablespoons balsamic vinegar

200 g (7 oz) Puy lentils

250 g (8 oz) cranberries, defrosted if frozen

2 bay leaves

salt and pepper

crusty bread, to serve

1 Preheat the slow cooker if necessary – see manufacturer's instructions. Heat the oil in a frying pan, add the sausages and fry over a high heat until browned all over, but not cooked through. Transfer to a plate.

2 Add the onion to the pan and fry, stirring, until lightly browned. Add the garlic, if using, then the flour. Stir in the stock, sugar, tomato purée and vinegar, season with salt and pepper and bring to the boil.

3 Put the lentils, cranberries and bay leaves in the slow cooker pot, pour in the hot stock mixture, then add the sausages. Cover with the lid and cook on 'Low' for 6–7 hours. Stir well, then spoon into shallow dishes, discarding the bay leaves, and serve with warmed crusty bread.

Pheasant with pancetta

This makes a smart dinner party dish. Creamy gratin Dauphinois and green beans are good accompaniments to serve.

Serves 4

Preparation time: 35 minutes
Cooking time: 2½–3 hours
Slow cooker size: standard

4 pheasant breasts, about 600 g (1 lb 3 oz)
small bunch of sage
100 g (3½ oz) packet of sliced
    smoked pancetta
25 g (1 oz) butter
200 g (7 oz) shallots, halved if large
2 tablespoons plain flour
150 ml (¼ pint) dry cider
150 ml (¼ pint) chicken stock
1 teaspoon Dijon mustard
1 dessert apple, cored and sliced
240 g (7¾ oz) can whole peeled chestnuts,
    drained
salt and pepper
chopped parsley, to garnish

1 Preheat the slow cooker if necessary – see manufacturer's instructions. Rinse the pheasant breasts with cold water, pat dry with kitchen paper, then season well with salt and pepper. Top each breast with a few sage leaves, then wrap in sliced pancetta until completely covered. Tie at intervals with fine string to keep the pancetta in place.

2 Heat the butter in a frying pan, add the shallots and fry for 4–5 minutes until browned. Stir in the flour, then add the cider, stock and mustard. Add the apple and chestnuts and a little extra salt and pepper, then bring to the boil, stirring.

3 Arrange the pheasant breasts in the slow cooker pot. Pour the hot cider mixture over the top. Cover with the lid and cook on 'Low' for 2½–3 hours until the pheasant is tender. Spoon on to plates, remove the string from the pheasant and garnish with chopped parsley.

Tip

Chicken breasts may be wrapped and cooked in the same way. Unlike pheasant breasts, they do not dry out as readily, so they can be left in the slow cooker for 5–6 hours without spoiling if you are delayed.

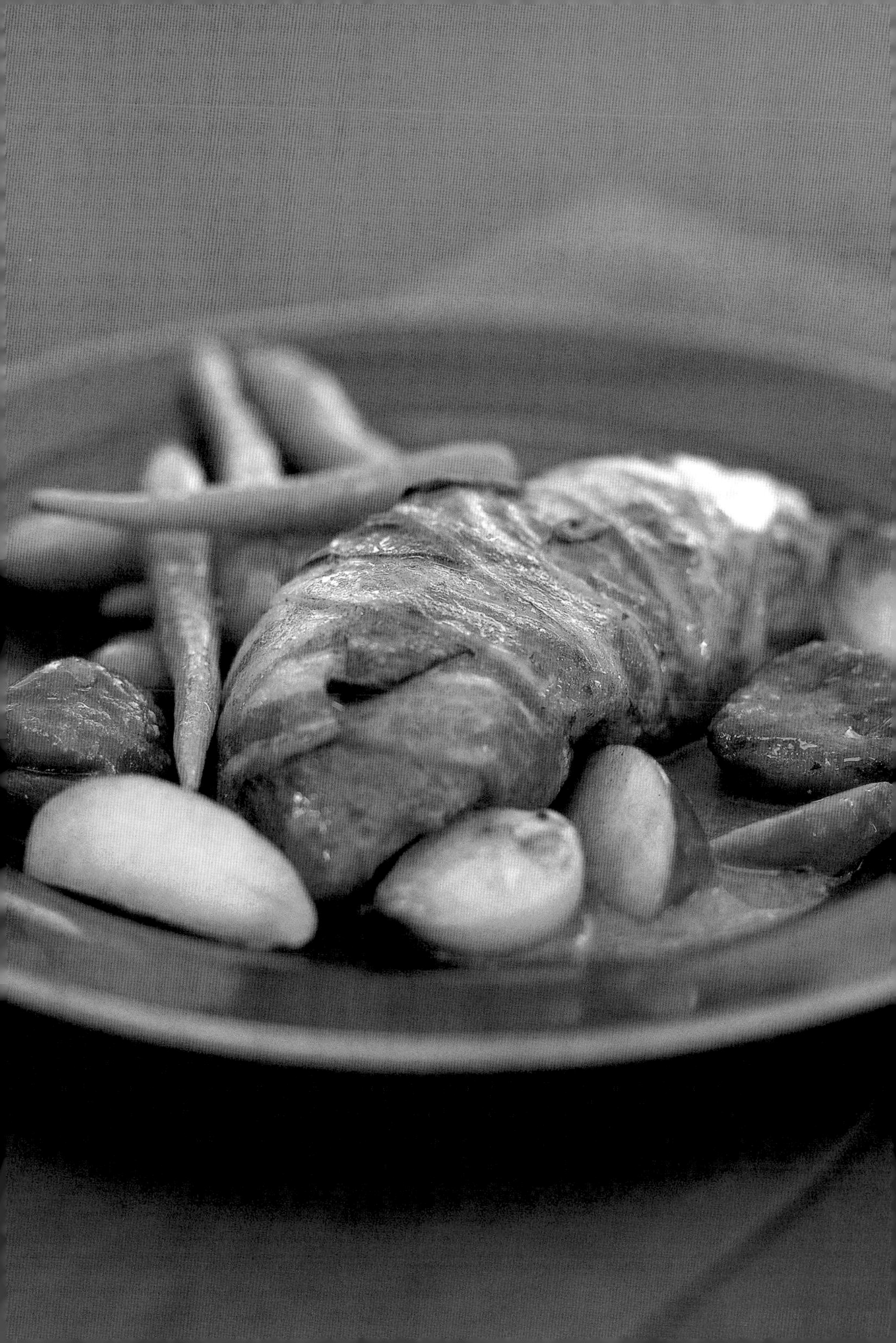

Cheat's game pie

Serves 6

Preparation time: 45 minutes
Cooking time: 8½–9½ hours
Slow cooker size: standard

15 g (½ oz) butter
1 tablespoon olive oil
1 cock pheasant, jointed
1 chicken leg, separated into drumstick and
    thigh joints
350 g (11½ oz) diced venison
1 large onion, chopped
100 g (3½ oz) smoked streaky bacon, rinded
    and diced
3 tablespoons brandy
200 ml (7 fl oz) red wine
300 ml (½ pint) chicken stock
2 teaspoons juniper berries
3 bay leaves
1 tablespoon tomato purée
4 teaspoons cornflour
salt and pepper

Pastry circles

500 g (1 lb) puff pastry, defrosted if frozen
beaten egg, to glaze
coarse sea salt, for sprinkling

1 Preheat the slow cooker if necessary – see manufacturer's instructions. Heat the butter and oil in a frying pan, add the pheasant and chicken joints and fry until browned all over. Transfer to a plate.

2 Add the venison, onion and bacon to the pan and fry for 5 minutes, stirring until browned. Add the brandy, bring to the boil then flame with a match, taking care to stand well back. When the flames have subsided, stir in the wine, stock, juniper berries, bay leaves and tomato purée and season with salt and pepper. Bring to the boil, stirring.

3 Arrange the pheasant and chicken in the slow cooker pot. Pour in the venison and stock mixture. Cover with the lid and cook on 'Low' for 8–9 hours until tender.

4 Remove the pheasant and chicken from the slow cooker pot, but keep the slow cooker switched on. Take the meat off the bones and return to the pot. Mix the cornflour to a smooth paste with a little cold water, then stir into the casserole. Replace the lid and cook for another 30 minutes.

5 Meanwhile, roll out the pastry thinly on a lightly floured surface and cut out 6 x 12 cm (5 inch) circles. Place on a greased baking sheet. Cut decorative leaf shapes from any trimmings and arrange on top of the pastry circles. Brush the pastry with egg, sprinkle with salt and bake in a preheated oven, 200°C (400°F), Gas Mark 6, for 8–10 minutes until well risen and golden.

6 Spoon the game casserole on to serving plates, discarding the bay leaves, and top with the pastry circles to serve.

Cassoulet

This French so-called 'peasant food' is made in the classic way with beans, diced pork, spicy sausage, tomatoes and rough red wine. Duck has been used instead of the traditional, more expensive goose.

Serves 4

Preparation time: 30 minutes
Cooking time: 8–9 hours
Slow cooker size: standard

4 small duck legs
250 g (8 oz) lean pork belly rashers, rinded and diced
1 large onion, chopped
2–3 garlic cloves, chopped
2 tablespoons plain flour
400 g (13 oz) can chopped tomatoes
200 ml (7 fl oz) red wine
100 ml (3½ fl oz) chicken stock
1 tablespoon soft light or dark brown sugar
2 teaspoons Dijon mustard
2 × 410 g (13½ oz) cans mixed beans, drained and rinsed
125 g (4 oz) piece of chorizo sausage, diced
1 fresh or dried bouquet garni
40 g (1½ oz) fresh breadcrumbs
salt and pepper
green salad, to serve

1 Preheat the slow cooker if necessary – see manufacturer's instructions. Dry-fry the duck legs in a frying pan until browned all over. Transfer to a plate. Pour off all but 1 tablespoon duck fat from the pan.

2 Add the diced pork and onion to the pan and fry for 5 minutes, stirring, until lightly browned. Stir in the garlic and flour. Add the canned tomatoes, wine, stock, sugar and mustard. Season with salt and pepper and bring to the boil, stirring.

3 Pour half the drained beans into the slow cooker pot. Arrange the duck pieces, chorizo and bouquet garni on top. Add the remaining beans, then pour in the pork and tomato mixture. Sprinkle with the breadcrumbs, then cover with the lid and cook on 'Low' for 8–9 hours. Spoon on to plates and serve with a green salad.

Tip

If your slow cooker has a maximum working capacity of less than 2.5 litres (4 pints), use 2 halved duck breasts and an extra 250 g (8 oz) diced pork belly, otherwise the mixture will not fit in the pot.

Vegetable dishes

Warm beetroot & brown bean salad

Amazingly tasty and yet made with just a few ingredients, this salad is served here as a simple vegetarian main course, but it could also be served in smaller portions as a delicious first course.

Serves 4–5

Preparation time: 25 minutes
Cooking time: 3½–4½ hours
Slow cooker size: standard

1 tablespoon olive oil
1 large onion, chopped
500 g (1 lb) raw beetroot, peeled and finely diced
2 x 410 g (13½ oz) cans borlotti beans, drained and rinsed
450 ml (¾ pint) vegetable stock
salt and pepper

To serve

¼ cucumber, finely diced
200 ml (7 fl oz) natural yogurt
1 cos or iceberg lettuce
4 red- or white-stemmed spring onions, thinly sliced
4 tablespoons chopped coriander or mint leaves
salt and pepper

1 Preheat the slow cooker if necessary – see manufacturer's instructions. Heat the oil in a frying pan, add the onion and fry, stirring, for 5 minutes until pale golden. Add the beetroot to the pan with the drained beans, stock and plenty of salt and pepper. Bring to the boil, stirring.

2 Transfer the beetroot mixture to the slow cooker pot. Cover with the lid and cook on 'Low' for 3½–4½ hours until the beetroot is tender. Stir well and lift the pot out of the cooker.

3 Stir the diced cucumber into the yogurt and season with salt and pepper. Separate the lettuce leaves and rinse with cold water, drain well, then arrange on 4 or 5 individual plates. Top with the warm beetroot salad, then add spoonfuls of the cucumber yogurt. Scatter sliced spring onions and coriander or mint over the top and serve at once.

Tip

Use dried beans instead of canned if you prefer – soak 200 g (7 oz) dried beans overnight, drain and rinse, then boil rapidly in a saucepan of boiling water for 10 minutes before draining and using as above.

Gingered chickpeas

Packed with protein, canned chickpeas are a healthy and economical storecupboard ingredient, used here to produce a supper dish ideally served with warmed pitta bread, plain rice or Coconut and Lime Rice (see page 37).

Serves 4
Preparation time: 15 minutes
Cooking time: 4–5 hours
Slow cooker size: standard

1 tablespoon olive oil
1 large onion, chopped
2 small parsnips, diced
2 carrots, diced
5 cm (2 inch) piece of fresh root ginger, finely chopped
1 teaspoon fennel seeds, roughly crushed
1 teaspoon turmeric
2 teaspoons paprika
400 g (13 oz) can chopped tomatoes
425 g (14 oz) can chickpeas, drained and rinsed
1 tablespoon soft light or dark brown sugar
600 ml (1 pint) hot vegetable stock
salt and pepper
torn coriander leaves, to garnish

1 Preheat the slow cooker if necessary – see manufacturer's instructions. Heat the oil in a frying pan, add the onion and fry, stirring, for 5 minutes until lightly browned. Add the diced parsnips and carrots and cook for 2–3 minutes.

2 Stir in the ginger, crushed fennel seeds, turmeric and paprika, then add the canned tomatoes, chickpeas, sugar and plenty of salt and pepper. Bring to the boil, then transfer to the slow cooker pot. Stir in the hot stock.

3 Cover with the lid and cook on 'Low' for 4–5 hours until the vegetables are tender. Spoon into shallow dishes, garnish with torn coriander leaves and serve.

Tip

This dish freezes well in individual portions ready to be reheated in the microwave.

Mushroom & cannellini bean stroganoff

Serves 4

Preparation time: 25 minutes, plus soaking
Cooking time: 2½–3 hours
Slow cooker size: standard

25 g (1 oz) dried porcini mushrooms
200 ml (7 fl oz) boiling water
25 g (1 oz) butter
1 tablespoon sunflower oil
1 large onion, chopped
3 celery sticks, sliced
250 g (8 oz) chestnut mushrooms, halved or
    quartered, depending on size
1–2 garlic cloves, crushed or chopped
    (optional)
3 tablespoons plain flour
200 ml (7 fl oz) dry white wine
150 ml (¼ pint) vegetable stock
2 teaspoons Dijon mustard
¼ teaspoon cayenne pepper
small bunch of thyme or a pinch of dried
410 g (13½ oz) can cannellini beans, drained
    and rinsed
salt
cayenne pepper or paprika, to garnish
soured cream, to serve

1 Put the dried mushrooms in a heatproof
bowl and cover with the boiling water. Leave
to soak for 20 minutes. Meanwhile, preheat the
slow cooker if required – see manufacturer's
instructions.

2 Heat the butter and oil in a frying pan. Add
the onion and fry until lightly browned. Stir in
the celery, fresh mushrooms and garlic, if using,
and cook for 2–3 minutes. Mix in the flour, then
gradually add the wine and stock. Stir in the
mustard, cayenne pepper and a little salt.
Reserve a couple of thyme sprigs to garnish,
then chop the rest and add to the pan together
with the reconstituted dried mushrooms and
their soaking liquid. Bring to the boil, stirring.

3 Pour the mushroom mixture into the slow
cooker pot, then stir in the beans. Cover with
the lid and cook on 'Low' for 2½–3 hours.
Spoon on to plates, sprinkle with thyme leaves
stripped from the reserved sprigs and serve,
topped with spoonfuls of soured cream and a
sprinkling of cayenne pepper or paprika.

Cauliflower balti

This mild curry is thickened towards the end of cooking with ground almonds. Serve it with warmed naan bread, which can be dunked in the sauce.

Serves 4

Preparation time: 25 minutes
Cooking time: 3¼–4¼ hours
Slow cooker size: standard

2 tablespoons sunflower oil
1 large onion, finely chopped
1 aubergine, diced
2 teaspoons cumin seeds, roughly crushed
2 teaspoons black mustard seeds
1 teaspoon turmeric
1 tablespoon mild curry paste
2–3 garlic cloves, chopped
400 g (13 oz) can chopped tomatoes
450 ml (¾ pint) vegetable stock
1 cauliflower, cut into medium-sized florets
1 baking potato, diced
3 tablespoons ground almonds
salt and pepper
coriander leaves, to garnish (optional)
naan bread, to serve

1 Preheat the slow cooker if necessary – see manufacturer's instructions. Heat the oil in a frying pan, add the onion and fry, stirring, for 5 minutes until lightly browned. Add the aubergine and fry for 3–4 minutes.

2 Stir in the spices, curry paste and garlic and cook for 1 minute. Add the canned tomatoes, stock and salt and pepper to taste and bring to the boil, stirring.

3 Put the cauliflower and potato in the slow cooker pot and add the tomato mixture. Cover with the lid and cook on 'High' for 3–4 hours until the vegetables are cooked. Stir in the ground almonds and cook for 15 minutes more. Ladle into shallow dishes, garnish with coriander leaves, if liked, and serve with warmed naan bread.

Chakchouka

Popular in North African countries, this ratatouille-style dish is finished by adding whole eggs towards the end of cooking so that they poach among the vegetables. Add some crushed dried chillies for a fiery kick, if liked.

Serves 4

Preparation time: 20 minutes
Cooking time: 3–3½ hours
Slow cooker size: standard

2 tablespoons olive oil
1 large onion, roughly chopped
2 red peppers, halved, cored, deseeded and cut into chunks
1 orange pepper, halved, cored, deseeded and cut into chunks
2 large courgettes, cut into large dice
2 garlic cloves, crushed
400 g (13 oz) can chopped tomatoes
2 teaspoons caster sugar
4 eggs
salt and pepper
crusty bread or garlic bread, to serve

1 Preheat the slow cooker if necessary – see manufacturer's instructions. Heat the oil in a frying pan, add the onion and fry, stirring, for 5 minutes until lightly browned. Add the peppers, courgettes and garlic and fry for 2 minutes. Stir in the canned tomatoes, sugar and salt and pepper to taste and bring to the boil.

2 Transfer the mixture to the slow cooker pot. Cover with the lid and cook for 2½–3 hours. Stir the mixture, then make 4 shallow indentations, slightly spaced apart, using a spoon. Crack an egg into each hollow, replace the lid of the slow cooker and cook for another 25–30 minutes until the egg whites are firm and the yolks still slightly soft. Spoon carefully on to serving plates and serve with warmed crusty bread or garlic bread.

Split pea sofrito

This is like a Middle Eastern version of dhal, in which the split peas soften and thicken the sauce as they cook. It is served with toasted bread croutes topped with a fiery harissa-flavoured butter.

Serves 4

Preparation time: 30 minutes, plus
*   overnight soaking*
Cooking time: 6–7 hours
Slow cooker size: standard

150 g (5 oz) split peas, soaked overnight
   in cold water
3 tablespoons olive oil
1 large onion, chopped
3 carrots, diced
½ teaspoon pimenton (smoked paprika)
750 ml (1¼ pints) vegetable stock
salt and pepper

Topping
75 g (3 oz) butter
2 teaspoons harissa
2 garlic cloves, crushed
2 tablespoons chopped mint
1 small French stick, sliced

1 Preheat the slow cooker if necessary – see manufacturer's instructions. Drain and rinse the soaked split peas. Heat the oil in a frying pan, add the onion and fry, stirring, for 5 minutes until lightly browned. Stir in the carrots and pimenton and cook for 1 minute.

2 Stir the split peas into the pan with the stock and season with salt and pepper. Bring to the boil, stirring, then cook for 2 minutes.

3 Pour the mixture into the slow cooker pot. Cover with the lid and cook on 'Low' for 6–7 hours. Meanwhile, make the spiced butter by beating the butter with the harissa in a shallow bowl. Mix in the garlic and mint, cover with clingfilm and chill until required.

4 Ladle the sofrito into shallow dishes and stir in a little of the spiced butter. Toast the slices of French bread and spread with the remaining spiced butter. Float the toasts on top of the sofrito and serve immediately.

Pumpkin & carrot cobbler

Serves 4

Preparation time: 45 minutes
Cooking time: 3–3½ hours
Slow cooker size: standard

1 tablespoon sunflower oil
1 large onion, chopped
500 g (1 lb) pumpkin or butternut squash,
  deseeded, peeled and diced
500 g (1 lb) carrots, diced
400 g (13 oz) can chopped tomatoes
250 ml (8 fl oz) vegetable stock
1 teaspoon caster sugar
2–3 rosemary sprigs or a pinch of dried
salt and pepper

Topping
150 g (5 oz) self-raising flour
pinch of salt
50 g (2 oz) butter, diced
75 g (3 oz) blue cheese, such as Stilton or
  Danish blue, rinded and diced
4 teaspoons finely chopped rosemary
  (optional)
4 tablespoons water

1 Preheat the slow cooker if necessary – see manufacturer's instructions. Heat the oil in a frying pan, add the onion and fry, stirring, for 5 minutes until lightly browned.

2 Add the pumpkin or butternut squash, carrots, canned tomatoes, stock, sugar and rosemary and season with salt and pepper. Bring to the boil, stirring.

3 Transfer the vegetable mixture to the slow cooker pot. Cover with the lid and cook on 'High' for 2½–3 hours until the vegetables are tender.

4 Meanwhile, make the topping: put the flour and salt in a mixing bowl. Rub in the butter until the mixture resembles fine breadcrumbs. Mix in the cheese and rosemary, if using, then stir in enough of the water to make a smooth, soft dough.

5 Pat the dough into a round 18 cm (7 inches) in diameter then cut into 8 segments. Arrange these on top of the vegetable mixture. Replace the cooker lid and cook for another 30 minutes until the pastry is well risen and puffy. If the slow cooker pot fits under your grill, brown the topping under a preheated grill before serving.

Pistachio & apricot pilaf

This is a good storecupboard supper, quickly put together before you collect the kids from school, or ideal to start cooking before younger children's bath and story time, ready for an adults–only supper later.

Serves 4

Preparation time: 25 minutes
Cooking time: 2½–3 hours
Slow cooker size: standard

1 tablespoon olive oil
1 large onion, chopped
75 g (3 oz) mixed pistachios, walnuts
   and hazelnuts
25 g (1 oz) sunflower seeds
200 g (7 oz) easy-cook brown rice
1 litre (1¾ pints) vegetable stock
75 g (3 oz) ready-to-eat dried apricots,
   chopped
25 g (1 oz) currants
1 cinnamon stick, halved
6 cloves
3 bay leaves
1 tablespoon tomato purée
salt and pepper
lightly toasted mixed nuts, to garnish

1 Preheat the slow cooker if necessary – see manufacturer's instructions. Heat the oil in a frying pan, add the onion and fry, stirring, for 5 minutes until lightly browned.

2 Add the nuts and seeds and fry until lightly browned. Stir in the rice and stock, followed by the dried fruit, spices, bay leaves and tomato purée, and season with salt and pepper to taste. Bring to the boil, stirring.

3 Transfer the mixture to the slow cooker pot. Cover with the lid and cook on 'Low' for 2½–3 hours until the rice is tender and the stock has been absorbed. Discard the cinnamon stick, cloves and bay leaves before serving, garnished with the lightly toasted nuts.

Sweet potato & chestnut jollof

Traditionally made with rice, this African-inspired dish has been made with pearl barley and flavoured with a little ground mace. It is topped with a coleslaw-style garnish.

Serves 4

Preparation time: 30 minutes
Cooking time: 4–5 hours
Slow cooker size: standard

1 tablespoon sunflower oil
1 large onion, chopped
½ teaspoon pimenton (smoked paprika) or
   chilli powder
500 g (1 lb) sweet potato, peeled and cut into
   chunks no larger than 1.5 cm (¾ inch)
240 g (7¾ oz) can whole peeled
   chestnuts, drained
100 g (3½ oz) pearl barley
¼ teaspoon ground mace
4 cloves
600 ml (1 pint) vegetable stock
1 tablespoon tomato purée
salt and pepper

To garnish
1 dessert apple, cored and finely chopped
1 small orange, segmented and chopped
125 g (4 oz) red or white cabbage, finely
   shredded
1 tablespoon finely chopped coriander

1 Preheat the slow cooker if necessary – see manufacturer's instructions. Heat the oil in a frying pan, add the onion and fry, stirring, for 5 minutes until lightly browned. Stir in the pimenton or chilli powder and cook for 1 minute.

2 Stir in the sweet potato, chestnuts, pearl barley, mace, cloves, stock, tomato purée and salt and pepper to taste and bring to the boil, stirring.

3 Transfer the mixture to the slow cooker pot. Cover with the lid and cook on 'Low' for 4–5 hours until the barley and potatoes are tender.

4 Combine the garnish ingredients. Spoon the jollof on to individual plates, top with the coleslaw mixture and serve.

Green bean risotto with pesto

Risottos are incredibly easy to make in a slow cooker and because they cook so gently they are unlikely to boil dry. Frozen vegetables have been used to save time, but fresh ones could be used if preferred.

Serves 4

Preparation time: 20 minutes
Cooking time: about 2–2½ hours
Slow cooker size: standard

25 g (1 oz) butter
1 tablespoon olive oil
1 onion, chopped
2 garlic cloves, chopped
250 g (8 oz) risotto rice
1.3 litres (2¼ pints) hot vegetable stock
2 teaspoons pesto
125 g (4 oz) extra fine frozen green beans
125 g (4 oz) frozen peas
salt and pepper

To garnish
Parmesan cheese shavings
basil leaves

1 Preheat the slow cooker if necessary – see manufacturer's instructions. Heat the butter and oil in a saucepan, add the onion and fry, stirring, for 5 minutes until softened and just beginning to brown.

2 Stir in the garlic and rice and cook for 1 minute. Add all but 150 ml (¼ pint) of the stock, season with salt and pepper, then bring to the boil. Transfer to the slow cooker pot, cover with the lid and cook on 'Low' for 2 hours.

3 Stir in the pesto and the remaining stock if some more liquid is needed. Place the frozen vegetables on top of the rice, then replace the lid and cook for another 20–30 minutes until the vegetables are hot. Serve, garnished with Parmesan shavings and basil leaves.

Tip

If you need to avoid dairy produce, replace the butter with a little extra olive oil, use fresh basil leaves instead of the pesto and drizzle with lemon juice instead of finishing with Parmesan.

Chilli black bean stew

These slow-cooked spicy beans get better the longer they are cooked. The stew is perfect for freezing in individual portions.

Serves 4–6

Preparation time: 30 minutes, plus
*   overnight soaking*
Cooking time: 8–10 hours
Slow cooker size: standard

250 g (8 oz) dried black beans, soaked
   overnight in cold water
2 tablespoons olive oil
1 large onion, chopped
2 carrots, diced
2 celery sticks, sliced
2–3 garlic cloves, chopped
1 teaspoon fennel seeds, crushed
1 teaspoon cumin seeds, crushed
2 teaspoons coriander seeds, crushed
1 teaspoon chilli powder or pimenton
   (smoked paprika)
400 g (13 oz) can chopped tomatoes
300 ml (½ pint) vegetable stock
1 tablespoon light soft or dark brown sugar
salt and pepper

Avocado salsa

1 avocado
grated rind and juice of 1 lime
½ red onion, finely chopped
2 tomatoes, diced
2 tablespoons chopped coriander leaves

To serve

150 g (5 oz) soured cream or natural yogurt
boiled rice or crusty bread

1 Preheat the slow cooker if necessary – see manufacturer's instructions. Drain and rinse the soaked beans. Place in a saucepan, add fresh water to cover and bring to the boil. Boil vigorously for 10 minutes, then drain the beans into a sieve.

2 Meanwhile, heat the oil in the saucepan, add the onion and fry, stirring, for 5 minutes until softened. Add the carrots, celery and garlic and fry for 2–3 minutes. Stir the crushed fennel and cumin seeds into the vegetables with the chilli powder or pimenton and cook for 1 minute.

3 Add the canned tomatoes, stock, sugar and a little pepper. Bring to the boil, then pour into the slow cooker pot. Mix in the beans, press under the liquid, then cover the pot and cook on 'Low' for 8–10 hours.

4 About 10 minutes before serving, make the avocado salsa: halve the avocado, remove the stone and peel away the skin. Dice the flesh, toss with the lime rind and juice, then mix with the onion, tomatoes and coriander.

5 Season the cooked beans to taste with salt, then serve, topped with spoonfuls of soured cream or yogurt and the avocado salsa, accompanied by boiled rice or crusty bread.

Fish & seafood

Squid in red wine

This squid, cooked slowly in the traditional Greek way with red wine and bay leaves, seems to almost melt in the mouth. Serve as a light lunch for four or as a starter for six people.

Serves 4

Preparation time: 25 minutes
Cooking time: 3½–4½ hours
Slow cooker size: standard

625 g (1¼ lb) prepared squid, defrosted
   if frozen
2 tablespoons olive oil
2 large onions, thinly sliced
375 g (12 oz) plum tomatoes, skinned if liked
   and roughly chopped
2–3 garlic cloves, chopped
2 bay leaves
2–3 rosemary sprigs
200 ml (7 fl oz) red wine
2 tablespoons red or white wine vinegar
2 teaspoons sugar
salt and pepper
crusty bread, to serve

1 Preheat the slow cooker if necessary – see manufacturer's instructions. Rinse the squid in plenty of cold water. Drain well, pull out the tentacles and put in a separate bowl. Cover and return to the refrigerator. Cut the body of the squid into 1 cm (½ inch) thick slices, then set aside.

2 Heat the oil in a frying pan, add the onions and fry, stirring, for 5 minutes until lightly browned. Add the tomatoes and garlic and cook for 2–3 minutes, then add the bay leaves, rosemary, wine, vinegar, sugar and plenty of salt and pepper.

3 Stir the sliced squid into the tomato mixture and bring to the boil. Transfer to the slow cooker pot, press the squid below the level of the liquid, then cover with the lid and cook on 'Low' for 3–4 hours.

4 Stir well, add the reserved squid tentacles and cook for 30 minutes more. Spoon the squid into shallow dishes and serve with plenty of warmed crusty bread to mop up the sauce.

Tips

One medium octopus can be used in place of the squid, but simmer in a saucepan of water for 1 hour before slicing and continuing with the recipe as above.

Stuffed monkfish with coriander & chilli

This meaty, lobster-like white fish is stuffed with a wonderfully refreshing mix of coriander, chilli and lime rind, and cooked with pak choi.

Serves 3–4

Preparation time: 40 minutes
Cooking time: about 2½ hours
Slow cooker size: standard oval-shaped

1 monkfish tail, about 875 g (1¾ lb)
small bunch of coriander
50 g (2 oz) butter
grated rind and juice of 1 lime
1–2 large mild red chillies, halved, deseeded
   and finely chopped
2 spring onions, thinly sliced
150 ml (¼ pint) hot fish stock
150 g (5 oz) pak choi, thickly sliced
salt and pepper
lime wedges, to garnish
white rice or soft noodles, to serve

1 Preheat the slow cooker if necessary – see manufacturer's instructions. Check that all the skin and thin membrane under the skin has been removed from the fish. Cut a slit along the length of the piece of fish and remove the central bone and attached fins.

2 Roughly chop 40 g (1½ oz) of the coriander leaves and beat into the butter with the lime rind, chopped chillies and spring onions. Spoon the mixture into the cavity of the fish and tie the fish neatly at intervals with fine string.

3 Arrange the fish in the slow cooker pot, bending it if necessary to fit. Season with salt and pepper and pour the stock around the fish. Cover with the lid and cook on 'Low' for 1½ hours. Turn the fish over and cook for 30–45 minutes more until it is opaque and flakes when pressed with a knife.

4 Add the pak choi to the slow cooker and press into the stock. Replace the lid and cook for another 15–25 minutes until just tender. Carefully transfer the fish to a shallow serving dish and remove the string. Drizzle with the lime juice and garnish with the remaining coriander. Spoon the pak choi around the fish and pour the remaining sauce into a separate bowl. Garnish with lime wedges and serve with white rice or soft noodles.

Crystal steamed trout

Serves 4

Preparation time: 30 minutes
Cooking time: 1 1/4–1 1/2 hours
Slow cooker size: extra large oval-shaped

4 small trout, about 1 kg (2 lb), gutted and
  heads removed
3.5 cm (1 1/2 inch) piece of fresh root ginger
1 carrot
4 spring onions
1/2 red pepper, cored and deseeded
juice of 1 lime
2 teaspoons sunflower oil
3 tablespoons sesame seeds
1 tablespoon soy sauce
2 limes, halved, to serve
egg-fried rice, to serve

1 Preheat the slow cooker if necessary – see manufacturer's instructions. Stand an upturned tea plate on an individual tart tin or a large biscuit cutter at the bottom of your slow cooker pot. Pour enough boiling water into the pot to come just below the plate.

2 Rinse the trout and lay them side by side on a large piece of buttered foil. Cut the ginger, carrot, spring onions and red pepper into thin strips. Tuck a few strips inside the trout cavities and sprinkle the rest over the top. Spoon the lime rind and juice over the trout.

3 Heat the oil in a frying pan, add the sesame seeds and cook for 2–3 minutes until browned. Remove from the heat, stir in the soy sauce, then spoon over the trout.

4 Fold the foil up and over the trout and seal the edges together well. Then carefully lower the foil parcel on to the plate in the slow cooker pot. Cover with the lid and cook on 'High' for 1 1/4–1 1/2 hours. To check that the fish is done, lift the foil parcel out of the cooker. Open the parcel out and press a knife into the inside of the trout – the flesh should flake easily when pressed.

5 Lift the trout out of the foil and transfer the foil parcel to a large serving plate. Serve with halved limes, to squeeze over the trout, and egg-fried rice.

Italian seafood casserole

Large, moist flakes of white fish, chunky pieces of mixed seafood and tiny pasta shapes make this tangy lemon- and tomato-based stew a hearty family meal in a bowl.

Serves 4

Preparation time: 30 minutes
Cooking time: 2 hours 20 minutes–3½ hours
Slow cooker size: standard

1 tablespoon olive oil
1 large onion, chopped
2 garlic cloves, chopped
400 g (13 oz) can chopped tomatoes
grated rind and juice of 1 lemon
450 ml (¾ pint) fish stock
1 tablespoon tomato purée
2 teaspoons caster sugar
500 g (1 lb) pollack, haddock or hake, skinned
    and cut into large chunks
1 red pepper, halved, cored, deseeded
    and diced
100 g (3½ oz) small pasta shells or macaroni
1 courgette, finely diced
100 g (3½ oz) frozen cooked peeled prawns,
    defrosted and rinsed (optional)
salt and pepper
basil leaves or pesto, to garnish
ciabatta or garlic bread, to serve

1 Preheat the slow cooker if necessary – see manufacturer's instructions. Heat the oil in a frying pan, add the onion and fry, stirring, for 5 minutes until lightly browned. Add the garlic, then the canned tomatoes, lemon rind and juice, stock, tomato purée, sugar and salt and pepper. Bring to the boil, stirring.

2 Place the fish in the slow cooker pot, add the red pepper and pasta, then cover with the tomato sauce. Cover the pot with the lid and cook on 'Low' for 2–3 hours until the fish and pasta are tender.

3 Turn the cooker setting to 'High'. Stir in the courgette and prawns, if using, and cook for 20–30 minutes until piping hot and the courgette is tender. Spoon into shallow dishes, sprinkle with basil leaves or pesto and serve with warmed ciabatta or garlic bread.

Swordfish bourride

Bourride is a traditional Mediterranean fish soup, similar to bouillabaisse. Using ready-prepared cooked mixed seafood makes it easy to prepare while the paprika and saffron add an extra kick.

Serves 4

Preparation time: 30 minutes
Cooking time: 1 hour 20 minutes–2 hours
Slow cooker size: standard

2 tablespoons olive oil
1 large onion, chopped
2–3 garlic cloves, crushed
1 teaspoon paprika
large pinch of saffron threads
3 plum tomatoes, skinned and chopped
4 tablespoons white wine
1 tablespoon tomato purée
2 teaspoons caster sugar
2 large swordfish or tuna steaks, about 625 g
    (1 1/4 lb), halved
200 g (7 oz) cooked mixed seafood – to
    include prawns, mussels and squid, defrosted
    if frozen and rinsed
salt and pepper

To serve
rouille (optional)
green salad
French bread

1 Preheat the slow cooker if necessary – see manufacturer's instructions. Heat the oil in a frying pan, add the onion and fry, stirring, for 5 minutes until lightly browned. Stir in the garlic and paprika and cook for 1 minute.

2 Add the saffron, tomatoes, wine, tomato purée, sugar and salt and pepper and bring to the boil, stirring.

3 Arrange the fish steaks in the slow cooker pot and pour the sauce over the top. Cover with the lid and cook on 'Low' for 1–1 1/2 hours until the fish is cooked through.

4 Turn the cooker setting to 'High', stir in the seafood and cook for 20–30 minutes more until piping hot. Spoon on to serving plates and serve topped with spoonfuls of rouille (mayonnaise mixed with finely chopped red chilli and garlic) if liked, a green salad and warmed French bread.

Tip

Don't be tempted to add extra liquid – it's surprising how much liquid there will be by the end of cooking.

Poached salmon with beurre blanc

A gently baking slow cooker is ideal for cooking larger pieces of fish. An oval-shaped cooker is best, although a round one will work perfectly well – just make sure that the fish fits in the cooker pot before you begin.

Serves 4

Preparation time: 25 minutes
Cooking time: 1½–1¾ hours
Slow cooker size: standard

100 g (3½ oz) butter
1 large onion, thinly sliced
1 lemon, sliced
500 g (1 lb) piece of thick end salmon fillet, no longer than 18 cm (7 inches)
1 bay leaf
200 ml (7 fl oz) dry white wine
150 ml (¼ pint) fish stock
3 tablespoons finely chopped chives, plus extra whole chives to garnish
salt and pepper
lemon slices, to garnish
new potatoes and a green salad, to serve

1 Preheat the slow cooker if necessary – see manufacturer's instructions. Brush inside the slow cooker pot with a little of the butter. Fold a large piece of foil into 3, then place at the bottom of the pot with the ends sticking up to use as a strap. Arrange the onion slices and half the lemon slices over the foil.

2 Place the salmon, flesh side uppermost, on top. Season with salt and pepper, then add the bay leaf and remaining lemon slices. Pour the wine and stock into a saucepan, bring to the boil, then pour over the salmon. Fold the foil down if necessary to fit the cooker lid, then cook on 'Low' for 1½–1¾ hours until the fish is opaque and flakes easily when pressed with a knife.

3 Lift the salmon carefully out of the pot using the foil strap, draining off as much liquid as possible. Place on a serving plate, discard the bay leaf and lemon and onion slices and keep warm. Strain the cooking liquid into a saucepan and boil rapidly for 4–5 minutes until reduced to about 4 tablespoons.

4 Reduce the heat and gradually whisk in small pieces of the remaining butter, little by little, until the sauce thickens and becomes creamy. (Don't be tempted to hurry making the sauce either by adding the butter in one go or by increasing the heat to the sauce, or you may find that it separates.) Stir in the chopped chives and adjust the seasoning if needed.

5 Cut the salmon into 4 portions, discard the skin and transfer to individual plates. Spoon a little of the sauce around the fish. Garnish with lemon slices and whole chives. Serve with new potatoes and a green salad.

Desserts

White chocolate bread & butter pudding

Serves 4–5

Preparation time: 35 minutes
Cooking time: 4–4 1/2 hours
Slow cooker size: standard, large or extra large

half a French stick, thinly sliced
50 g (2 oz) butter, at room temperature
100 g (3 1/2 oz) white chocolate, chopped
4 egg yolks
50 g (2 oz) caster sugar, plus 3 tablespoons
   extra for caramelizing
150 ml (1/4 pint) double cream
300 ml (1/2 pint) milk
1 teaspoon vanilla essence

Blueberry coulis

125 g (4 oz) blueberries
1 tablespoon caster sugar
4 tablespoons water

To decorate (optional)

a few extra blueberries
a little white chocolate, diced

1 Preheat the slow cooker if necessary – see manufacturer's instructions. Spread the slices of French bread with the butter. Layer the bread in a 1.2 litre (2 pint) heatproof soufflé dish that will fit comfortably in your slow cooker pot (allowing for a gap of at least 1.5 cm/3/4 inch all the way around), sprinkling the chopped white chocolate between the layers of bread.

2 Beat the egg yolks and sugar together in a heatproof bowl with a fork. Pour the cream and milk into a saucepan and bring just to the boil. Gradually stir into the egg mixture, then stir in the vanilla essence.

3 Pour the cream mixture over the layered bread slices and leave to stand for 10 minutes.

4 Cover the top of the soufflé dish with foil, then lower into the slow cooker pot, using foil straps or a string pudding bowl lifter (see page 9). Pour hot water around the dish to come halfway up the side, then cover the cooker with the lid and cook on 'Low' for 4–4 1/2 hours until the custard has set.

5 Meanwhile, make the blueberry coulis: purée the blueberries with the sugar and water until smooth. Pour into a jug and set aside.

6 Carefully lift the dish out of the slow cooker. Remove the foil and sprinkle the remaining sugar over the top of the pudding. Caramelize the sugar under a hot grill or using a cook's blowtorch. To serve, spoon the bread and butter pudding into individual bowls and sprinkle with extra blueberries and white chocolate, if using. Stir the blueberry coulis and pour it around the pudding.

Figgy pudding with cinnamon custard

This is real comfort food, a sweet suet pudding dotted with moist figs and apricots and lightened with breadcrumbs and orange juice. Use vegetable suet if you are cooking for vegetarians.

Serves 6

Preparation time: 30 minutes
Cooking time: 3–3¼ hours
Slow cooker size: standard, large or extra large

butter, for greasing
6 tablespoons golden syrup
150 g (5 oz) self-raising flour
½ teaspoon bicarbonate of soda
1 teaspoon ground cinnamon
100 g (3½ oz) shredded suet
50 g (2 oz) fresh breadcrumbs
175 g (6 oz) ready-to-eat dried figs, chopped
50 g (2 oz) ready-to-eat dried apricots, chopped
grated rind and juice of 1 orange
2 eggs, beaten

Cinnamon custard
425 g (14 oz) can ready-made custard
¼ teaspoon ground cinnamon
2–3 tablespoons sherry

1 Preheat the slow cooker if necessary – see manufacturer's instructions. Lightly butter a 1.2 litre (2 pint) pudding basin that will fit comfortably in your slow cooker pot and line the bottom with a circle of nonstick baking or greaseproof paper. Spoon in 2 tablespoons of the golden syrup.

2 Put the flour, bicarbonate of soda, cinnamon, suet and breadcrumbs in a mixing bowl and mix together. Add the dried fruit, orange rind and juice, eggs and remaining golden syrup and mix.

3 Spoon the pudding ingredients into the bottom of the prepared basin. Cover with buttered and pleated foil, tie with string and make a string handle. Stand the pudding basin on an upturned saucer in the slow cooker pot, then pour boiling water around the basin to come halfway up its side. Add the cooker lid and cook on 'High' for 3–3¼ hours. Lift the pudding out of the slow cooker and check that it is cooked. It should be well risen and browned, and the top should spring back when pressed with a fingertip.

4 To serve, heat the custard ingredients together in a saucepan, stirring until smooth. Remove the string and foil from the pudding, run a knife around the inside edge of the basin to loosen the pudding, then turn it out on to a plate. Remove the lining paper and serve with the hot custard.

Jewelled rice pudding

This quickly made, nursery-style dessert is for those who are definitely not on a diet! For an extra special touch, soak the dried fruits in a little sherry or orange liqueur for 2–3 hours or overnight before using.

Serves 6

Preparation time: 10 minutes
Cooking time: 4–4½ hours
Slow cooker size: standard

butter, for greasing
900 ml (1½ pints) full-fat milk
75 g (3 oz) pudding rice
75 g (3 oz) caster sugar
1½ teaspoons vanilla essence
50 g (2 oz) ready-to-eat dried apricots, chopped
50 g (2 oz) dried berries and cherries (a mix of dried cranberries, blueberries and cherries)
grated nutmeg, for sprinkling
extra thick cream and red berry jam, to serve

1 Preheat the slow cooker if necessary – see manufacturer's instructions. Brush the cooker pot with a little butter. Pour the milk into a saucepan, bring just to the boil, then pour into the cooker pot.

2 Add the rice, sugar and vanilla essence then stir in the dried fruit. Sprinkle the top with the nutmeg. Cover with the lid and cook on 'Low' for 4–4½ hours until the rice is tender. Don't leave the pudding to cook for any longer as you may find that the milk begins to separate.

3 To serve, spoon the rice pudding into individual bowls and top with spoonfuls of extra thick cream and red berry jam.

Sticky orange sponge pudding with orange sauce

Serves 4–6

Preparation time: 35 minutes
Cooking time: 3–3 ½ hours
Slow cooker size: standard, large or extra large

2 oranges, unpeeled
250 ml (8 fl oz) water
125 g (4 oz) butter, at room temperature, plus
   extra for greasing
200 g (7 oz) caster sugar
3 eggs, beaten
175 g (6 oz) self-raising flour
¼ teaspoon ground cinnamon
3 tablespoons golden syrup
1 tablespoon cornflour

1 Thinly slice 1 of the oranges. Grate the rind and squeeze the juice from the other. Put the sliced orange in a saucepan with the water, cover and simmer for 20 minutes until the orange is tender.

2 Meanwhile, preheat the slow cooker if necessary – see manufacturer's instructions. Butter the inside of a 1.2 litre (2 pint) pudding basin. Put the remaining butter and 125 g (4 oz) of the sugar in a mixing bowl and beat until light and fluffy using a wooden spoon or an electric mixer. Gradually beat the eggs and flour alternately into the creamed mixture, then stir in half the orange rind and the ground cinnamon.

3 Lift the cooked orange slices out of the water, reserving the water, then arrange enough slices to cover the bottom and side of the pudding basin. Spoon in the golden syrup. Add the creamed mixture and smooth the surface flat.

4 Cover with buttered and pleated foil. Tie tightly in place with string, adding a string handle. Stand the basin on an upturned saucer in the slow cooker pot, then pour boiling water into the pot to come halfway up the sides of the basin. Cover with the lid and cook on 'High' for 3–3½ hours.

5 Meanwhile, make the orange sauce: measure the reserved orange water and juice and make up to 250 ml (8 fl oz) with extra water. Finely chop any remaining cooked orange slices and stir into the juice with the remaining orange rind and sugar. Mix the cornflour to a smooth paste with a little cold water in a saucepan. Add the juice mixure. Bring the sauce to the boil, stirring until thickened and smooth. Strain, if liked.

6 Remove the string and foil from the basin – the pudding should be well risen and the top should spring back when pressed with a fingertip. Run a knife around the inside edge of the basin to loosen the pudding, then turn it out on to a plate. Cut into wedges and serve with the warm orange sauce.

Baked vanilla cheesecake

Serves 6

Preparation time: 45 minutes, plus
*   overnight chilling*
Cooking time: 3 hours
Slow cooker size: large or extra large

Base

50 g (2 oz) butter, at room temperature
50 g (2 oz) caster sugar
50 g (2 oz) self-raising flour
1 egg

Cheesecake

300 g (10 oz) full-fat cream cheese
200 ml (7 fl oz) full-fat crème fraîche
50 g (2 oz) caster sugar
3 eggs, beaten
1 teaspoon vanilla essence
icing sugar, to decorate
mixed berry fruits, to serve

1 Preheat the slow cooker if necessary – see manufacturer's instructions. Line the base and side of an 18 cm (7 inch) diameter, deep round cake tin with nonstick baking paper – do not use a loose-bottomed tin. Put all the ingredients for the base in a mixing bowl or food processor and beat together until smooth. Spoon into the prepared cake tin, smooth with a knife, then cover the top of the tin loosely with foil.

2 Stand the cake tin on an upturned individual tart tin, saucer or large biscuit cutter in the slow cooker pot. Pour boiling water into the pot to come halfway up the side of the cake tin, then add the lid and cook on 'High' for 1 hour.

3 Meanwhile, make the cheesecake: put the cream cheese, crème fraîche and sugar in a bowl. Gradually mix in the eggs until smooth, then stir in the vanilla essence.

4 Carefully lift the cake tin out of the slow cooker pot using oven gloves. Carefully remove the foil – the sponge layer should be dry and able to be pressed with a fingertip. Pour the cheesecake mixture into the tin on top of the cooked sponge, cover again loosely with foil and return to the slow cooker pot. Replace the lid and cook on 'High' for 2 hours until the cheesecake is firm enough to be touched lightly with the fingertips.

5 Switch off the slow cooker, remove the foil and leave the cheesecake to cool, still in the hot water. Don't be alarmed to see that the cheesecake will sink on cooling – this is normal. When the water is barely warm, lift the tin out, cover with clingfilm and transfer to the refrigerator. Chill overnight to achieve the characteristic baked cheesecake texture.

6 Carefully remove the cheesecake from the cake tin, peel off the lining paper and place on a serving plate. Dust liberally with icing sugar and serve with mixed berry fruits.

Classic crème brûlée

Crack through the thin, brittle caramelized sugar topping to reveal a rich and velvety vanilla custard. Although this dessert is served in all the posh restaurants, it is surprisingly easy to make at home, especially in a slow cooker.

Serves 4

Preparation time: 30 minutes, plus chilling
Cooking time: 3–3 ½ hours
Slow cooker size: standard, large or extra large

½ vanilla pod
400 ml (14 fl oz) double cream
5 egg yolks
40 g (1½ oz) caster sugar
2 tablespoons icing sugar, for caramelizing
selection of berry fruits, to serve

1 Preheat the slow cooker if necessary – see manufacturer's instructions. Slit the vanilla pod along its length, then place in a saucepan with the cream. Bring the cream just to the boil, then remove from the heat and leave for 20 minutes to allow the flavours to infuse.

2 Mix the egg yolks and sugar together in a bowl using a fork. Lift the vanilla pod out of the cream, scrape the black seeds away from inside the pod with a small, sharp knife and add them to the cream. Reheat the cream until almost boiling, then gradually stir into the egg mixture. Strain into a jug.

3 Pour the mixture into 4 x 150 ml (¼ pint) heatproof ramekin dishes, then stand the dishes in the slow cooker pot – there is no need to cover them with foil. Pour hot water around the dishes to come halfway up their sides, taking care not to splash any water into the cream. Cover the cooker with the lid and cook on 'Low' for 3–3½ hours until the desserts are set, with a slight quiver to their centres.

4 Carefully lift the cooker pot out of the base unit using oven gloves. Leave to cool at room temperature, then lift the ramekin dishes out and transfer to the refrigerator for at least 4 hours until well chilled.

5 Just before serving, sprinkle the top of the desserts with icing sugar (there is no need to sift it), then caramelize the sugar using a cook's blowtorch. If you don't have a blowtorch, arrange the ramekin dishes in a small roasting tin, half-fill it with cold water and add ice cubes. Place the tin under a hot grill, getting the tops of the ramekin dishes as close to the heat as you can, to caramelize the sugar topping.

6 To serve, stand the ramekin dishes on small plates and decorate with berry fruits. Serve within 20 minutes.

Poached peaches with marsala & vanilla

Fresh peaches are delicious eaten raw, but can go mouldy quickly. Capture them at their best by cooking them in this Italian-inspired sugar syrup, flavoured with marsala and vanilla, for an effortless but elegant dessert.

Serves 4–6

Preparation time: 15 minutes
Cooking time: 1¼–1¾ hours
Slow cooker size: standard

150 ml (¼ pint) marsala or sweet sherry
150 ml (¼ pint) water
75 g (3 oz) caster sugar
6 firm ripe peaches or nectarines, halved
   and pitted
1 vanilla pod, slit lengthways
2 teaspoons cornflour
125 g (4 oz) fresh raspberries
crème fraîche, to serve

1 Preheat the slow cooker if necessary – see manufacturer's instructions. Put the marsala or sherry, the water and sugar in a saucepan and bring to the boil.

2 Place the peach or nectarine halves and vanilla pod in the slow cooker pot and pour in the hot syrup. Cover with the lid and cook on 'Low' for 1–1½ hours until hot and tender.

3 Lift the fruit out of the slow cooker pot and place in a serving dish. Remove the vanilla pod, then scrape the black seeds from the pod with a small, sharp knife and stir the seeds back into the cooking syrup. Mix the cornflour to a smooth paste with a little cold water, then stir into the cooking syrup and cook on 'High' for 15 minutes, stirring occasionally.

4 Pour the thickened syrup over the peaches, sprinkle with the raspberries and serve warm or chilled with spoonfuls of crème fraîche.

Tips

This dish is equally delicious served with vanilla ice cream or mascarpone cheese, or with whipped cream flavoured with crushed amaretti or ratafia biscuits.

To make in a larger slow cooker, increase the ingredient quantities by half as much again.

Triple chocolate cake

Serves 6–8

Preparation time: 40 minutes
Cooking time: 2–2½ hours
Slow cooker size: large or extra large

50 g (2 oz) cocoa powder
6 tablespoons boiling water
175 g (6 oz) self-raising flour
1½ teaspoons baking powder
150 g (5 oz) caster sugar
150 ml (¼ pint) sunflower oil
3 eggs

To finish

4 tablespoons chocolate and hazelnut spread
450 ml (¾ pint) double cream
white chocolate curls
a little sifted cocoa powder

1 Preheat the slow cooker if necessary – see manufacturer's instructions. Line the bottom and side of an 18 cm (7 inch) diameter, deep round cake tin with nonstick baking paper – do not use a loose-bottomed tin. Put the cocoa in a small bowl and gradually mix to a smooth paste with the boiling water. Leave to cool.

2 Put the flour, baking powder and sugar in a mixing bowl and mix well. Beat together the oil and eggs, then add to the dry ingredients. Spoon in the cocoa paste and mix together until smooth.

3 Pour the cake mixture into the prepared cake tin, smooth with a knife, then cover the top of the tin loosely with foil. Stand the cake tin on an upturned saucer or individual tart tin in the slow cooker pot. Pour boiling water into the pot to come halfway up the side of the cake tin. Cover with the lid and cook on 'High' for 2–2½ hours or until the cake is well risen, the top is dry and a skewer inserted into the centre comes out clean.

4 Carefully lift the cake tin out of the slow cooker pot using oven gloves. Remove the cake from the tin and turn it out on to a wire rack. Peel off the lining paper and leave to cool.

5 Just before serving, split the cake into 3 layers. Place the bottom layer on a serving plate and spread with half the chocolate and hazelnut spread. Whip the cream until it just holds its shape, spoon a little of the cream over the chocolate spread and smooth with a knife. Top with another cake layer and spread with more chocolate spread and cream. Add the last layer of cake and spread the remaining cream over the top and sides of the cake. Sprinkle with white chocolate curls and dust with a little cocoa.

Dark chocolate pots with coffee cream liqueur

This dessert is simple to create, yet wonderfully decadent. Do check that the small pots or mugs fit in your slow cooker before you begin. Use milk chocolate instead of dark if you prefer.

Serves 4

Preparation time: 25 minutes, plus chilling
Cooking time: 3–3 ½ hours
Slow cooker size: standard, large or extra large

450 ml (¾ pint) full-fat milk
150 ml (¼ pint) double cream
200 g (7 oz) dark chocolate, broken
   into pieces
2 whole eggs
3 egg yolks
50 g (2 oz) caster sugar
¼ teaspoon ground cinnamon

Topping

150 ml (¼ pint) double cream
75 ml (3 fl oz) coffee cream liqueur
chocolate curls, to decorate

1 Preheat the slow cooker if necessary – see manufacturer's instructions. Pour the milk and cream into a saucepan and bring just to the boil. Remove from the heat, add the chocolate pieces and set aside for 5 minutes, stirring occasionally until the chocolate has melted.

2 Put the whole eggs, egg yolks, sugar and cinnamon in a mixing bowl and whisk until smooth. Gradually whisk in the warm chocolate milk, then strain the mixture into 4 x 250 ml (8 fl oz) heatproof pots or mugs.

3 Cover the tops of the pots or mugs with foil, then stand them in the slow cooker pot. Pour hot water into the slow cooker pot to come halfway up the sides of the pots or mugs. Cover the cooker with the lid and cook on 'Low' for 3–3½ hours until set.

4 Carefully lift the dishes out of the slow cooker pot using oven gloves. Leave to cool at room temperature, then transfer to the refrigerator for at least 4 hours until well chilled.

5 Just before serving, whip the cream until soft swirls form. Gradually whisk in the liqueur, then spoon the flavoured cream over the top of the desserts. Sprinkle with chocolate curls and serve.

Plum & polenta cake

This continental-style cake, which doubles as a dessert if served with cream, is made with ground almonds and polenta instead of wheat flour, so is ideal for anyone on a wheat-free diet.

Serves 6

Preparation time: 30 minutes
Cooking time: 3–3 1/2 hours
Slow cooker size: large or extra large

150 g (5 oz) butter, at room temperature, plus extra for greasing
200 g (7 oz) sweet red plums, thickly sliced
150 g (5 oz) caster sugar
2 eggs, beaten
100 g (3 1/2 oz) ground almonds
50 g (2 oz) fine polenta (cornmeal)
1/2 teaspoon baking powder
grated rind and juice of 1/2 orange
whipped cream, to serve (optional)

To decorate
2 tablespoons toasted flaked almonds
sifted icing sugar

1 Preheat the slow cooker if necessary – see manufacturer's instructions. Butter a 1.2 litre (2 pint) oval or round heatproof dish that will fit comfortably in your slow cooker pot and line the bottom with a piece of nonstick baking or greaseproof paper. Arrange the plum halves, cut side down, in rings in the base of the dish.

2 Beat the remaining butter and sugar together in a mixing bowl until light and fluffy. Gradually beat the eggs and ground almonds alternately into the creamed mixture. Stir in the polenta, baking powder, orange rind and juice and beat until smooth.

3 Spoon the cake mixture over the plums and smooth with a knife. Cover the dish with buttered foil, then stand it on an upturned saucer or 2 individual tart tins in the slow cooker pot. Pour boiling water into the pot to come halfway up the side of the dish. Add the cooker lid, then cook on 'High' for 3–3 1/2 hours or until the top of the cake is dry and springs back when pressed with a fingertip.

4 Carefully remove the dish from the slow cooker using oven gloves. Take off the foil and leave to cool slightly, then run a knife around the inside edge of the dish to loosen the cake and turn it out on to a serving plate. Remove the lining paper, sprinkle the top with toasted flaked almonds and dust with a little sifted icing sugar to decorate. Cut into wedges and serve warm or cold with spoonfuls of whipped cream, if liked.

Chutneys, conserves & drinks

Chillied tomato & garlic chutney

Perk up a simple ham or cheese sandwich with this tasty chutney. If you are not a fan of spicy food, then simply leave out the chillies, but if you like your food extra hot, use the chilli seeds as well.

Tip

Don't worry if your slow cooker pot is very full as the tomatoes will quickly lose their bulk once cooking begins.

Makes 5 x 400 g (13 oz) jars

Preparation time: 30 minutes
Cooking time: 6–8 hours
Slow cooker size: standard

1 kg (2 lb) tomatoes, skinned and roughly chopped
1 large onion, chopped
2 cooking apples, about 500 g (1 lb), peeled, cored and chopped
2 red peppers, halved, cored, deseeded and diced
75 g (3 oz) sultanas
100 ml (3½ fl oz) distilled malt vinegar
250 g (8 oz) granulated sugar
2–3 large mild red chillies, halved, deseeded and finely chopped
6–8 garlic cloves, finely chopped
1 cinnamon stick, halved
½ teaspoon ground allspice
1 teaspoon salt
pepper

1 Preheat the slow cooker if necessary – see manufacturer's instructions. Put all the ingredients in the slow cooker pot, mix together, then cover with the lid and cook on 'High' for 6–8 hours until thick and pulpy.

2 Warm 5 clean jars in the bottom of a low oven. Spoon in the chutney, place a waxed disc on top and leave to cool. Seal each jar with a screw-topped lid, then label. Store in a cool place for up to 2 months. Once opened, store in the refrigerator.

Spiced mango chutney

This sweet, fruity chutney can be partnered with cheese for a tasty salad or served with poppadums and raita to start a spicy Indian meal.

Makes 3 x 400 g (13 oz) jars

Preparation time: 30 minutes
Cooking time: 2½–2¾ hours
Slow cooker size: standard

1 large mango
1 small butternut squash, about 750 g (1½ lb), deseeded, peeled and diced
2 large onions, chopped
200 g (7 oz) soft light brown sugar
100 ml (3½ fl oz) white wine vinegar
3.5 cm (1½ in) piece of fresh root ginger, peeled and finely chopped
1 teaspoon cumin seeds, roughly crushed
2 teaspoons coriander seeds, roughly crushed
1 teaspoon black onion seeds
1 teaspoon turmeric
1 teaspoon salt
pepper

1 Preheat the slow cooker if necessary – see manufacturer's instructions. Cut a thick slice off the sides of the mango to reveal the large, flat oval stone. Peel, then dice all the flesh.

2 Put the mango, butternut squash and onions in the slow cooker pot and mix in the sugar and vinegar. Add the ginger, crushed cumin and coriander seeds, black onion seeds and turmeric and season with salt and pepper. Cover with the lid and cook on 'High' for 2½–2¾ hours until thick.

3 Warm 3 clean jars in the bottom of a low oven. Spoon in the chutney, place a waxed disc on top and leave to cool. Seal each jar with a screw-topped lid, then label. Store in a cool place for up to 2 months. Once opened, store in the refrigerator.

Pickled plums

**Makes 2 x 750 ml (1¼ pint) jars and
1 x 500 ml (17 fl oz) le parfait jar**

Preparation time: 20 minutes
Cooking time: 2–2½ hours
Slow cooker size: standard

750 ml (1¼ pints) white wine vinegar
500 g (1 lb) caster sugar
7 rosemary sprigs
7 thyme sprigs
7 small bay leaves
4 lavender sprigs (optional)
4 garlic cloves, unpeeled
1 teaspoon salt
½ teaspoon peppercorns
1.5 kg (3 lb) firm red plums, washed and pricked

Tip

Add a tiny dried chilli to each
jar of plums or add some broken
cinnamon sticks, juniper berries and
pared orange rind in place of the
fresh herbs. As the plums are stored,
so they will slightly lose colour.

1 Preheat the slow cooker if necessary – see
manufacturer's instructions. Pour the vinegar
and sugar into the cooker pot, then add 4 each
of the rosemary and thyme sprigs and the bay
leaves, all the lavender, if using, the garlic cloves,
salt and peppercorns. Cook on 'High' for 2–2½
hours, stirring once or twice.

2 Warm the 3 clean jars in the bottom of a
low oven. Pack the plums tightly into the jars.
Tuck the remaining fresh herbs into the jars.
Strain in the hot vinegar, making sure that the
plums are completely covered, then seal tightly
with rubber seals and jar lids.

3 Label the jars and leave to cool. Transfer to
a cool, dark cupboard and store for 3–4 weeks
before using. Once opened, store the pickled
plums in the refrigerator.

Chutneys, conserves & drinks 117

Tangy citrus curd

A variation on lemon curd, this recipe uses lime and orange as well to create a delicious breakfast or teatime spread for toast, fruit scones or crumpets. Use 3 lemons instead of the citrus mix to make lemon curd.

Makes 2 x 400 g (13 oz) jars
Preparation time: 25 minutes
Cooking time: 3–4 hours
Slow cooker size: standard, large or extra large

125 g (4 oz) unsalted butter
400 g (13 oz) caster sugar
grated rind and juice of 2 lemons
grated rind and juice of 1 orange
grated rind and juice of 1 lime
4 eggs, beaten

Tip

A jar of homemade fruit curd makes a great present. Decorate the top of the jar by tying a circle of brown paper or double square of muslin or patterned fabric in place with raffia or ribbon. Finish by adding a new teaspoon and a gift tag.

1 Preheat the slow cooker if necessary – see manufacturer's instructions. Put the butter and sugar in a saucepan, add the fruit rinds, then strain in the juice. Heat gently for 2–3 minutes, stirring occasionally, until the butter has melted and the sugar dissolved.

2 Pour the mixture into a basin that will fit comfortably in your slow cooker pot. Leave to cool for 10 minutes, then gradually strain in the eggs and mix well. Cover the basin with foil, put foil straps or a string pudding bowl lifter (see page 9) in the slow cooker pot and place the basin on top. Pour hot water into the cooker pot to come halfway up the side of the basin. Add the cooker lid and cook on 'Low' for 3–4 hours until the mixture is very thick. Stir once or twice during cooking if possible.

3 Warm 2 clean jars in the bottom of a low oven. Spoon in the citrus curd, place a waxed disc on top and leave to cool. Seal each jar with a screw-topped lid or a cellophane jam pot cover and an elastic band, label and store in the refrigerator. Use within 3–4 weeks.

Blackberry & apple jam

This softly set, French-style jam is made with less sugar than usual. Because timings are not so crucial in a slow cooker, this recipe is a good introduction to jam making. Blackcurrants, raspberries or mulberries could be used instead of blackberries.

Makes 4 x 400 g (13 oz) jars

Preparation time: 20 minutes
Cooking time: 4–5 hours
Slow cooker size: standard

1 kg (2 lb) cooking apples, peeled, cored
   and chopped
500 g (1 lb) granulated sugar
grated rind of 1 lemon
2 tablespoons water or lemon juice
250 g (8 oz) blackberries

1 Preheat the slow cooker if necessary – see manufacturer's instructions. Put all the ingredients in the slow cooker pot, in the order listed below. Cover with the lid and cook on 'High' for 4–5 hours, stirring once or twice during cooking. By the end of the cooking time the fruit should be thick and pulpy.

2 Warm 4 clean jars in the bottom of a low oven. Spoon in the jam, place a waxed disc on top and leave to cool. Seal each jar with a cellophane jam pot cover and an elastic band, label and store for up to 2 months in the refrigerator. The jam's low sugar content means that it does not keep as long as conventional jam and must be kept in the refrigerator.

Lemon cordial

Keep this cordial in the door of the refrigerator, then dilute as required with cold water or sparkling mineral water and lots of ice. Wonderfully refreshing, it is free from unnecessary additives. Tartaric acid is available from pharmacies.

Makes about 20 glasses

Preparation time: 10 minutes
Cooking time: 3–4 hours
Slow cooker size: standard

3 lemons, washed and thinly sliced
625 g (1¼ lb) granulated sugar
900 ml (1½ pints) boiling water
25 g (1 oz) tartaric acid
mint or lemon balm sprigs,
   to decorate (optional)
ice cubes, to serve

1 Preheat the slow cooker if necessary – see manufacturer's instructions. Add the lemon slices to the slow cooker pot with the sugar and boiling water, stir well until the sugar is almost all dissolved, then cover with the lid and cook on 'High' for 1 hour.

2 Reduce the heat and cook on 'Low' for 2–3 hours until the lemons are almost translucent. Switch off the slow cooker and stir in the tartaric acid. Leave to cool.

3 Remove and discard some of the sliced lemons using a slotted spoon. Transfer the cordial and remaining lemons to 2 sterilized screw-topped, wide-necked bottles or storage jars. Seal well, label and store in the refrigerator for up to 1 month.

4 To serve, dilute the cordial with water in a ratio of 1:3, adding a few of the sliced lemons for decoration, ice cubes and sprigs of mint or lemon balm, if available.

Spiced citrus cup

Warming and refreshing, this non-alcoholic punch is perfect for any guests who have to drive home. Vary the combination of fruit teas and spices to suit your taste. Try mixing cranberry, elderflower and raspberry tea with cranberry juice or perhaps camomile and elderflower tea with crushed coriander seeds and orange juice.

Makes 8–10 glasses

Preparation time: 10 minutes
Cooking time: 2–3 hours
Slow cooker size: standard

6 lemon and ginger or lemon and camomile
   herbal infusion tea bags
1.5 litres (2½ pints) boiling water
150 g (5 oz) caster sugar
3 tablespoons thick set honey
300 ml (½ pint) orange juice (from a carton)
2 cinnamon sticks, halved
10 cardamom pods, crushed
1 orange, sliced

1 Preheat the slow cooker if necessary – see manufacturer's instructions. Put the tea bags in the slow cooker pot. Pour in the boiling water, then add the sugar, honey, orange juice, cinnamon sticks, cardamom pods and their black seeds and sliced orange. Mix the ingredients together.

2 Cover with the lid and cook on 'Low' for 2–3 hours. Strain, if liked, to remove the tea bags and spices, then ladle into glasses.

Mulled cranberry & red wine

This is a great alcoholic beverage for winter entertaining but equally enjoyable at bonfire parties or late-night open-air summer concerts, poured from a vacuum flask.

Makes 8–10 glasses

Preparation time: 10 minutes
Cooking time: 4–5 hours
Slow cooker size: standard

75 cl bottle inexpensive red wine
600 ml (1 pint) cranberry juice
    (from a carton)
100 ml (3½ fl oz) brandy, rum, vodka or
    orange liqueur
100 g (3½ oz) caster sugar
1 orange
8 cloves
1–2 cinnamon sticks, depending on size

To serve

1 orange
8–10 long rosemary sprigs
2–3 bay leaves
a few fresh cranberries

1 Preheat the slow cooker if necessary – see manufacturer's instructions. Pour the red wine, cranberry juice and brandy or other alcohol into the slow cooker pot then stir in the sugar.

2 Cut the orange into 8 segments and stud each piece with a clove. Break the cinnamon sticks into large pieces and add to the pot with the orange pieces. Cover with the lid and cook on 'High' for 1 hour. Reduce the temperature and cook on 'Low' for 3–4 hours.

3 To serve, replace the orange with new pieces and add the rosemary sprigs, bay leaves and cranberries. Ladle into heatproof glasses, keeping back the fruit and herbs if liked.

Index

Acknowledgements

The author and publisher would like to thank Morphy Richards for loaning a range of different sized slow cookers for the testing and photography of this book. For further information, visit the Morphy Richards website on www.morphyrichards.co.uk or write to Morphy Richards, Talbot Road, Mexborough, South Yorkshire, S64 8AJ. They would also like to thank Prima for supplying a range of slow cookers for photography. For further information, write to Prima, Prima House, Premier Park, Oulton, Leeds, LS26 8ZA.

Executive Editor: Sarah Ford
Editor: Emma Pattison
Design Manager: Tokiko Morishima
Designer: Mark Stevens
Photographer: Stephen Conroy
Home Economist: Sara Lewis
Stylist: Claire Hunt
Senior Production Controller: Manjit Sihra